FORGIVENESS

FORGIVENESS

THE STORY OF EVA KOR, SURVIVOR OF THE AUSCHWITZ TWIN EXPERIMENTS

JOE LEE

RED ⚡ LIGHTNING BOOKS

This book is a publication of

Red Lightning Books
1320 East 10th Street
Bloomington, Indiana 47405 USA

redlightningbooks.com

Manufactured in the United States of America

First printing 2021

Cataloging information is available from the
Library of Congress.

ISBN 978-1-68435-178-7

To Eva Mozes Kor
This is not my story but hers.
I hope I have done her justice.

To her family,
Her husband, Mickey, who has his own story
    of survival and thriving,
Her daughter, Rina,
And to her son, Alex, who was always there.

And to her creation,
the CANDLES Holocaust Museum
    and Education Center
in Terre Haute, Indiana,
That continues her work.

CONTENTS

Preface

History sometimes becomes personal, not just something you read about in dusty books. It can be touched and touch you. It becomes real—not just images floating from a page or a screen but a small woman speaking forcefully about her lived experience standing right before your eyes. Living, breathing history. That was Eva.

Before there was Eva for me there was my father. I am the child of a disabled World War II veteran. Charles R. Lee, a mechanic with the Third Armored Division of the First Army. He went ashore on Normandy a few days after D-Day with gunfire and artillery still crackling in the air. He was at the Battle of the Bulge. Breeching the Siegfried Line. And also at the liberation of Nordhausen (officially Mittelbau-Dora), a Nazi concentration camp. It wasn't a death camp but one where labor and cruelty killed you, not the machinery of genocide in operation at Auschwitz and Birkenau.

Dad told of seeing the dead stacked like cordwood, of the living prisoners hollow-eyed and rail-thin croaking their thanks, touching the prayed-for dream of the liberating American GIs.

He told of his general, Maurice Rose, one of the few Jewish commanding officers (and one beloved by his men), having the local people march to and through the camp to see what many swore they had not seen, had not known. How the locals then dug the graves and buried the dead of that awful place.

The memory of my father's experience stayed with me, grew with books and films, and then there was Eva.

My wife, Bess, an art teacher and a recipient of Eli Lilly Teacher Renewal Grants was leading art workshops as part of the Lilly Extending Teacher Creativity summer programs held at Indiana State University in Terre Haute, Indiana, and joined with fellow teachers for one of Eva's talks at the CANDLES

Holocaust Museum and Education Center. She called me as soon as it was finished and insisted that I hear this little dynamo speak.

Time has its way of intervening, and we weren't able to go and hear Eva until the Saturday after Thanksgiving of 2018. In the meanwhile, we had visited dear friends in Pittsburgh, where my friend Mark Best introduced me to a local comic book project, "Chutz-Pow!," that was recording Holocaust survivor experiences in comic book form. Knowing what I did of Eva's experience and her profound and compassionate response to it, I started to think—what about a complete graphic biography telling the entire story of her life? So, with illustration packet and curriculum vitae in hand, I finally got to have the Eva experience.

Eva appeared using her wheeled walker to help push her feet forward. She had assistance taking the low stage in front of a large photo of the main gate of Auschwitz-Birkenau. Seated, she began speaking.

What she had to say is covered in the pages to follow, but one cannot capture the spirit of this indomitable woman. She was loving, feisty, funny, forceful, and completely commanded her audience. No cardboard saint, but a real and totally approachable hero—one who could snap back with a pithy reply as well as a loving hug. Truly, one of a kind.

I met Eva, and knowing that I was one of many who wanted to meet her, only mentioned I had a project in mind for both us. The project I presented to Leah Simpson, the executive director of the museum, subsequently sending sample pages and gaining an approval to go forward. Eva did wonder if she was going to be made into a "superhero," and I assured everyone that no spandex would be required.

Every year, Eva and the museum take groups of people to tour Auschwitz. I pondered whether I should go on the trip scheduled for the beginning of July 2019. My wife assured me that if I was ever going to go now was the time (and she was so right). I applied and received an Individual Artist Grant from the Indiana Arts Commission that helped greatly with travel expenses (and earned my undying thanks) and traveled with a group of teachers, healthcare givers, and other seekers to this place both horrific and holy. I would urge everyone to go with a CANDLES group—you will be changed.

It was on this trip that Eva on the morning of July 4 died.

Some of that final day is described in subsequent pages, but as difficult as that day and the rest of our journey became without our guiding spirit, we all were reinforced with Eva's message and her command to *forgive*, to look life straight in the eye, and to do what we can to never let anything like the Holocaust ever happen again. She urged us to use her story as a vehicle to convey that message. This is my attempt to do so.

ACKNOWLEDGMENTS

There are many to thank for this book becoming a reality. If it takes a village to raise a child, it takes no less to produce a book.

First let me acknowledge some of those who have gone before me in telling Eva's story: the wonderful book that Eva co-authored with Lisa Rojany Buccieri, *Surviving the Angel of Death: The True Story of a Mengele Twin in Auschwitz*, and Ted Greene's inspiring documentary, *Eva – 7063*, most importantly. These are invaluable resources of Eva's life. There are also many articles, recordings, and videos of Eva and her story; just put her name into an internet search, and you will find much to enlighten and explore.

Next let me thank the CANDLES Holocaust Museum and Education Center, Eva's creation centered in Terre Haute, Indiana. This little facility not only houses a wealth of information about Eva and the Mengele twins as well as the Holocaust in general but is also a guiding source of compassion for all who have suffered oppression and trauma. It isn't just a candle but a beacon glowing with the power of Eva's core message of forgiveness.

The people who light that beacon every day are the museum's staff. The staff I worked specifically with are Catie Hahn, the development coordinator; Amber Maze, the education and program coordinator; Jessica McDonald, the former marketing and advertising manager; Beth Nairn, the former trip coordinator; and a special thanks to Leah Simpson, the executive director. They all have assisted me in this work even when they didn't know they were assisting.

It was my privilege to be one of the pilgrims on that fateful trip to Poland in July of 2019, and I couldn't have gotten there without a generous Individual Artist Grant from the Indiana Arts Commission. Thanks so much to the IAC and State

Representative Matt Pierce and former state senator Mark Stoops for always supporting the arts.

On that journey I made many friends and just to mention a special few: Megan and Chad Wallace, Joseph Lutz, Nancy and Charlie Cunov, Fred Bloom, Allison Cleary, and Maggie Baumgart. And all my other companions who shared, commiserated, and learned.

I should not fail to mention my dear friend Rachel Rosolina, who just happens to work at IU press and got this work into editors David Hulsey, Lesley Bolton, and Anna Francis's hands.

Finally, I should always and forever thank my wife, Bess. Without her cheering, cajoling, and love, this journey I have been on not just to Auschwitz and this book, but for the last twenty-three years would never have happened. And ditto to my kid, Brandon, who keeps me honest.

FORGIVENESS

CHAPTER 1: HOW COULD THIS HAPPEN?

AIRPLANES.

TANKS.

POISON GAS.

THE WAR TO END ALL WARS IS WHAT THEY CALLED WORLD WAR I.
A GENERATION OF YOUNG MEN KILLED, MAIMED, AND PSYCHOLOGICALLY SCARRED. IN TOTAL NINE MILLION SOLDIERS AND SEVEN MILLION CIVILIANS DIED IN THE CONFLICT, AND THAT WAS FOLLOWED BY THE INFLUENZA THAT KILLED FIFTY TO ONE HUNDRED MILLION PEOPLE WORLDWIDE.
HOW COULD WE EVER LET IT HAPPEN AGAIN?

No! This time humanity had learned its lesson and would never, ever again go down that catastrophic path to all-out conflict. And then World War II began less than thirty years later.

World War I began with an assassination in June 1914 that led to new alliances and the German and Austro-Hungarian Empire declaring war against France and Russia. Great Britain entered the war to protect France, and the United States followed in 1917.

When it ended in 1918, the victorious Allied Powers wanted to ensure that Teutonic aggression would not happen again and forced Germany to accept the Treaty of Versailles: reparations (equalling about $442 billion in today's currency), disarmament, and acceptance as the aggressors (the War Guilt Clause). Germany grudgingly signed considering it a "stab in the back".

2

IN 1919, THE ENTIRE POLITICAL MAKEUP OF GERMANY CHANGED. KAISER WILHELM II ABDICATED.

A NEW CONSTITUTION WAS WRITTEN, AND THE WEIMAR REPUBLIC WAS CREATED. BUT THE NEW GOVERNMENT COULD NOT DEFEAT THE EFFECTS OF WAR.

HYPERINFLATION AND THEN IN 1929 THE GREAT DEPRESSION RIPPED THE ECONOMY APART. UNEMPLOYMENT WAS RAMPANT, EASILY VISIBLE IN THE DISFIGURED, DISILLUSIONED VETERANS WHO BEGGED ON CITY STREET CORNERS.

RIVAL POLITICAL FACTIONS POWERED BY THUGS BATTLED FOR INFLUENCE IN ALLEYS AND SCREAMED SPEECHES IN PUBLIC SQUARES. SOCIALISTS, COMMUNISTS, AND THE NEW RISING PARTY, THE NATIONAL SOCIALIST WORKERS' PARTY (FORMED IN 1921) WITH ITS LEADER, ADOLF HITLER, AT THE HELM, DEBATED POLITICS WITH SPIT, FISTS, AND CLUBS.

IN 1923, HITLER AND HIS *NAZI* PARTY WENT FURTHER THAN ORATORY AND GANG VIOLENCE WHEN THEY ATTEMPTED TO TAKE OVER THE ENTIRE GOVERNMENT. THE BEER HALL PUTSCH BEGAN IN A MUNICH RATHSKELLER AND ENDED WITH HITLER IMPRISONED IN LANDSBERG PRISON.

TIME USED BY HITLER TO PEN HIS MANIFESTO OF ARYAN IDEOLOGY (THE RACIST MYTH OF A PURE, SUPERIOR, WHITE PEOPLE), ANTI-SEMITISM, HATRED, AND DOMINATION: *MEIN KAMPF* (MY STRUGGLE).

RELEASED IN 1924, THE FAILED ARTIST WHO HAD AT ONE TIME CONTEMPLATED BECOMING A PRIEST, THE WOUNDED WWI DISPATCH RUNNER, THE FORMERLY HOMELESS NE'ER-DO-WELL WHO HAD A GIFT FOR SPEECH-MAKING PUBLISHED HIS TESTAMENT OF POISON AND WITH HIS THUGGISH BROWN SHIRTS AT HIS ELBOW, BLUDGEONED HIS WAY FURTHER AND FURTHER UP THE LADDER OF POWER IN THE CRUMBLING REPUBLIC.

IN 1933, THE OLD AND AILING PRESIDENT PAUL VON HINDENBURG, WHO ALSO HAD THE DISTINCTION OF BEING GERMANY'S FAILED COMMANDING GENERAL IN WWI, APPOINTED HITLER CHANCELLOR.

CONVENIENTLY, THE REICHSTAG, THE SEAT OF GERMAN GOVERNMENT, CAUGHT FIRE AND IMMEDIATELY AFTER THE EMERGENCY ACT WENT INTO EFFECT AND CIVIL RIGHTS WERE SUSPENDED ACROSS THE NATION. HITLER BEGAN TO RUTHLESSLY SOLIDIFY POWER. THE FIRST CONCENTRATION CAMPS WERE SET UP ALMOST IMMEDIATELY TO IMPRISON LABOR ORGANIZERS AND OTHER POLITICAL RIVALS.

THE NIGHT OF THE LONG KNIVES PURGED THE SA (STURMABTEILUNG OR STORM TROOPS) OF ANY OFFICERS WHO MIGHT STAND IN OPPOSITION. HITLER USED THE SS (SCHUTZSTAFFEL OR SECURITY SQUADRON) TO CARRY OUT THE VIOLENCE, AND HE WOULD LATER HAVE IT PURGED OF ANY DISSIDENT ELEMENTS. THE WEHRMACHT (DEFENSE FORCE) WOULD UNDERGO CLEANSING IN 1938.

ON HINDENBURG'S DEATH THE FOLLOWING YEAR, CHANCELLOR HITLER BECAME THE FÜHRER, THE SUPREME LEADER OF THE GERMAN PEOPLE. BY THE TIME AN ELECTION WAS HELD BRIEFLY AFTER, THE NEWLY DUBBED FÜHRER GARNERED 88 PERCENT OF THE VOTE.

STIMME

HITLER QUICKLY EXPANDED THE NAZI ATROCITY.

IN 1935, THE NUREMBERG "RACIAL HYGIENE" LAWS WERE ENACTED, BARRING THE MARRIAGE OR ANY SEXUAL CONTACT BETWEEN ARYANS AND JEWS. LATER, THE LAWS WERE BROADENED TO EXCLUDE CONTACT WITH ROMA (GYPSIES) AND OTHER PEOPLE OF COLOR AS WELL.

ON NOVEMBER 6, 1937, IMPERIAL JAPAN (WHICH WAS ALREADY BRUTALLY MAKING WAR ON CHINA, KOREA, AND MUCH OF EAST ASIA) FORGED AN ALLIANCE WITH GERMANY AND FASCIST ITALY UNDER THE DICTATOR BENITO MUSSOLINI. THE TRIPARTITE PACT SOLIDIFIED THE AXIS POWERS. IN 1940, HUNGARY JOINED THE PACT AND THE TENTACLES OF TOTALITARIANISM WOULD EXTEND THROUGH MOST OF CONQUERED EUROPE.

IN 1938, THE ANSCHLUSS, THE FORCED REUNION OF GERMAN-SPEAKING PEOPLES, WOULD BEGIN WITH AUSTRIA AND THEN MOVE TO THE SUDETENLAND OF CZECHOSLOVAKIA.

IN NOVEMBER 1938, KRISTALLNACHT (THE NIGHT OF BROKEN GLASS) SHATTERED THE UNEASY SLEEP OF JEWISH MERCHANTS WHEN BANDS OF ARMED BRUTES SMASHED SHOP WINDOWS AND THE BONES OF THOSE WHO TRIED TO STOP THEM. THOUSANDS OF JEWS WERE ARRESTED FOR SIMPLY BEING JEWS.

SEPTEMBER 1939 SAW THE FIRST OFFICIAL ACT OF THE GERMAN GOVERNMENT MURDERING THE INNOCENT. AKTION T4 OR ACTION BRANDT LEGALIZED THE EUTHANASIA OF THE MENTALLY AND PHYSICALLY DISABLED FOR THE "GOOD OF THE STATE." ASYLUMS, HOSPITALS, AND REST HOMES BECAME EXECUTION CHAMBERS.

UNDER THE DOCTRINE OF LEBENSRAUM (LIVING SPACE) GERMAN ARMIES INVADED POLAND IN SEPTEMBER OF 1939. THE SLAVIC PEOPLES WERE CONSIDERED UNTERMENSCHEN (SUBHUMANS) AND NOT WORTHY OF THE LAND THEY OCCUPIED AND THEREFORE RIPE FOR CONQUEST.

GREAT BRITAIN AND FRANCE DECLARED WAR, UNABLE TO CONTINUE THEIR SILENCE IN THE FACE OF THE NAZI BLITZKRIEG (LIGHTNING WAR) AGAINST A PEACEFUL EUROPEAN NEIGHBOR.

IN 1940, THE GERMAN WAR MACHINE ROLLED OVER DENMARK, NORWAY, LUXEMBOURG, AND THE NETHERLANDS AND WAS PURSUING THE CAPITULATION OF FRANCE.

ON DECEMBER 7, 1941, JAPANESE AIRCRAFT ATTACKED THE UNSUSPECTING AMERICAN NAVAL BASE OF PEARL HARBOR IN HONOLULU, HAWAII. THE UNITED STATES DECLARED WAR ON JAPAN AND ITS ALLIES THE FOLLOWING DAY. THE ENTIRE WORLD WAS NOW AT WAR.

GERMANY BROUGHT BLOODY WAR TO ITS NEIGHBORS BUT ALSO TO THE INNOCENTS SINGLED OUT BY HITLER'S AGENDA OF HATE: JEWS, ROMA, POLES AND OTHER SLAVIC PEOPLES, JEHOVAH'S WITNESSES, SEVENTH-DAY ADVENTISTS, HOMOSEXUALS, COMMUNISTS, THE DISABLED, TRADE UNIONISTS, AND LATER, AFTER GERMANY DECLARED WAR ON THE SOVIET UNION (ENDING STALIN'S U.S.S.R.'s BRIEF FLING AS A NONCOMBATANT), SOVIET PRISONERS OF WAR. THIS LIST IS ONLY A PARTIAL ONE BECAUSE IT EXPANDED TO INCLUDE ANYONE WHO DISSENTED AND ANYONE WHO COULD NOT CONFORM TO THE NAZIS' VIEWS OF RACIAL OR IDEOLOGICAL PURITY.

FIRST CAME THE GHETTOS AND THEN THE CONCENTRATION CAMPS FILLED WITH PEOPLE PULLED FROM THEIR HOMES AND TRANSPORTED BY TRAIN, TYPICALLY CATTLE CARS, TO ISOLATED BARBED WIRE ENCLOSURES AND STACKED INTO BARRACKS LITTLE MORE THAN ANIMAL BARNS.

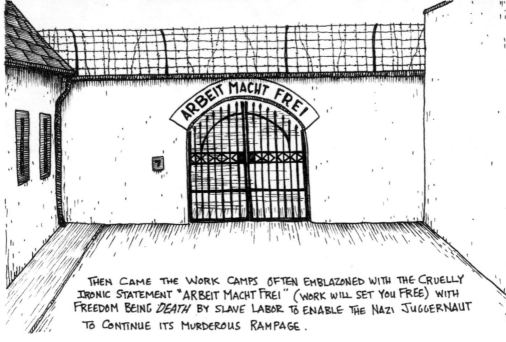

THEN CAME THE WORK CAMPS OFTEN EMBLAZONED WITH THE CRUELLY IRONIC STATEMENT "ARBEIT MACHT FREI" (WORK WILL SET YOU FREE) WITH FREEDOM BEING *DEATH* BY SLAVE LABOR TO ENABLE THE NAZI JUGGERNAUT TO CONTINUE ITS MURDEROUS RAMPAGE.

IN JANUARY OF 1942, THE NAZIS' WANNSEE CONFERENCE FORMALIZED THE "FINAL SOLUTION," THE DEATH CAMPS WITH THE SOLE PURPOSE OF KILLING THE JEWS AND ALL THOSE OTHERS DEEMED UNDESIRABLE. A BUREAUCRATIC GATHERING OF THE UPPER ECHELONS OF GERMAN GOVERNMENT AND MILITARY WHOSE JOB WAS TO CODIFY (BUT SUBTLY) THE DESTRUCTION OF INNOCENT LIVES AND CREATE A EUROPE TO BE INHABITED COMPLETELY BY THE ARYAN RACE. (BETWEEN 1939 AND 1945 THIS *DEMOCIDE* KILLED AT THE VERY LEAST SEVENTEEN MILLION GUILTLESS MEN, WOMEN, AND CHILDREN OF EVERY AGE WITH OVER SIX MILLION BEING JEWS.)

THE COUNTRY OF
ROMANIA UNDER
THE RULE OF
KING CAROL II
REMAINED NEUTRAL

UNTIL A COUP IN 1940
INSTALLED MARSHAL
ION ANTONESCU.

THE WAR HAD ONLY NIBBLED
AT THE EDGES OF THE COUNTRY,
BUT WITH THE FALL OF THE MONARCHY,
THE NAZIS MOVED IN, WITH
NORTHERN TRANSYLVANIA
BEING UNDER THE CONTROL
OF THE FASCIST HUNGARIANS
FROM 1940 TO 1944.

GERMANY
OCCUPIED HUNGARY
AND ITS TERRITORIES
DURING OPERATION
MARGARETHE IN 1944.
APPROXIMATELY 555,000 JEWS
WERE ROUNDED UP FROM EVEN
THE SMALLEST VILLAGES AND
TRANSPORTED PRIMARILY TO THE
EXTERMINATION CAMP AUSCHWITZ-
BIRKENAU IN POLAND WITH MOST BEING
FORCED ON ARRIVAL INTO THE GAS CHAMBERS.

Eva Mozes at ten years of age and her family were taken in Operation Margarethe.

CHAPTER 2: PORTZ

It's a girl!

JANUARY 31, 1934.

And another girl!

ALEXANDER MOZES WAS NOT OVERJOYED.

ALREADY HE HAD TWO GIRLS, EDIT AND ALIZ. HE LOVED THEM AND HE WOULD LOVE THESE TWIN DAUGHTERS, BUT WHY COULDN'T HE HAVE A SON?

JAFFA, ALEXANDER'S WIFE, WAS OVERJOYED! TWINS! WHAT FUN TO HAVE THESE NEW PRECIOUS DOLLS: MIRIAM AND EVA.

THE MOZES FAMILY, THE ONLY JEWISH FAMILY IN PORTZ, TRANSYLVANIA, A SECTION OF ROMANIA VERY CLOSE TO THE BORDER OF HUNGARY, HAD A FARM AT THE EDGE OF THE SMALL VILLAGE.

THE FARM HAD COWS, SHEEP, CHICKENS, AND GEESE.

A FLOWER GARDEN IN THE FRONT OF THE HOUSE

AND A KITCHEN GARDEN IN THE BACK.

A VINEYARD AND ORCHARDS OF APPLES, PLUMS, PEACHES, AND THREE VARIETIES OF CHERRIES.

SO MUCH FRUIT THE GIRLS WOULD SOMETIMES DRESS UP IN IT, BUT FRUIT WAS NOT HOW MAMA DRESSED THEM.

MAMA DRESSED THE LITTLE TWINS IN BEAUTIFUL MATCHING DRESSES.

BUT EVEN GARBED LIKE A STORYBOOK PRINCESS ON A MUSIC BOX, EVA WAS EVER READY TO BATTLE FOR DOING THINGS HER OWN WAY

SHE WOULD TRAVEL TO SZÉPLAK, A NEIGHBORING TOWN WITH AN ACCOMPLISHED SEAMSTRESS, TO FASHION STYLISH ENSEMBLES OF BURGUNDY, PINK, AND POWDER BLUE.

AND NOT IN SOME PRECONCEIVED NOTION OF THE WAY A LITTLE GIRL SHOULD BEHAVE.

18

PAPA ALEXANDER, A HARDWORKING FARMER AND PRACTITIONER OF HIS FAITH, HAD WANTED A BOY. A BOY COULD AS AN ORTHODOX JEW PROUDLY PARTICIPATE

IN PUBLIC WORSHIP; SAY THE KADDISH, A PRAYER RECITED IN THE SYNAGOGUE FOR THANKSGIVING, PRAISE, AND AT TIMES OF DEATH; BE PART OF A MINYAN, A GROUP OF TEN MEN NEEDED FOR DIFFERENT TYPES OF RELIGIOUS OBLIGATIONS; AND MOST IMPORTANT TO CARRY THE MOZES FAMILY NAME INTO THE FUTURE.

NO! TWO MORE GIRLS, SWEET MIRIAM, AND EVA! HEADSTRONG, REBELLIOUS, AND ALWAYS IN TROUBLE. A STRONG, DETERMINED, AND TROUBLEMAKING GIRL. WHAT COULD A FATHER DO BUT TRY TO CONTROL THIS WILD CHILD, THIS *VILDE CHAYA*. HE MUST SET BOUNDARIES AND ENFORCE THEM.

EVA JUST HAD TO BREAK THEM... AND SUFFER THE CONSEQUENCES.

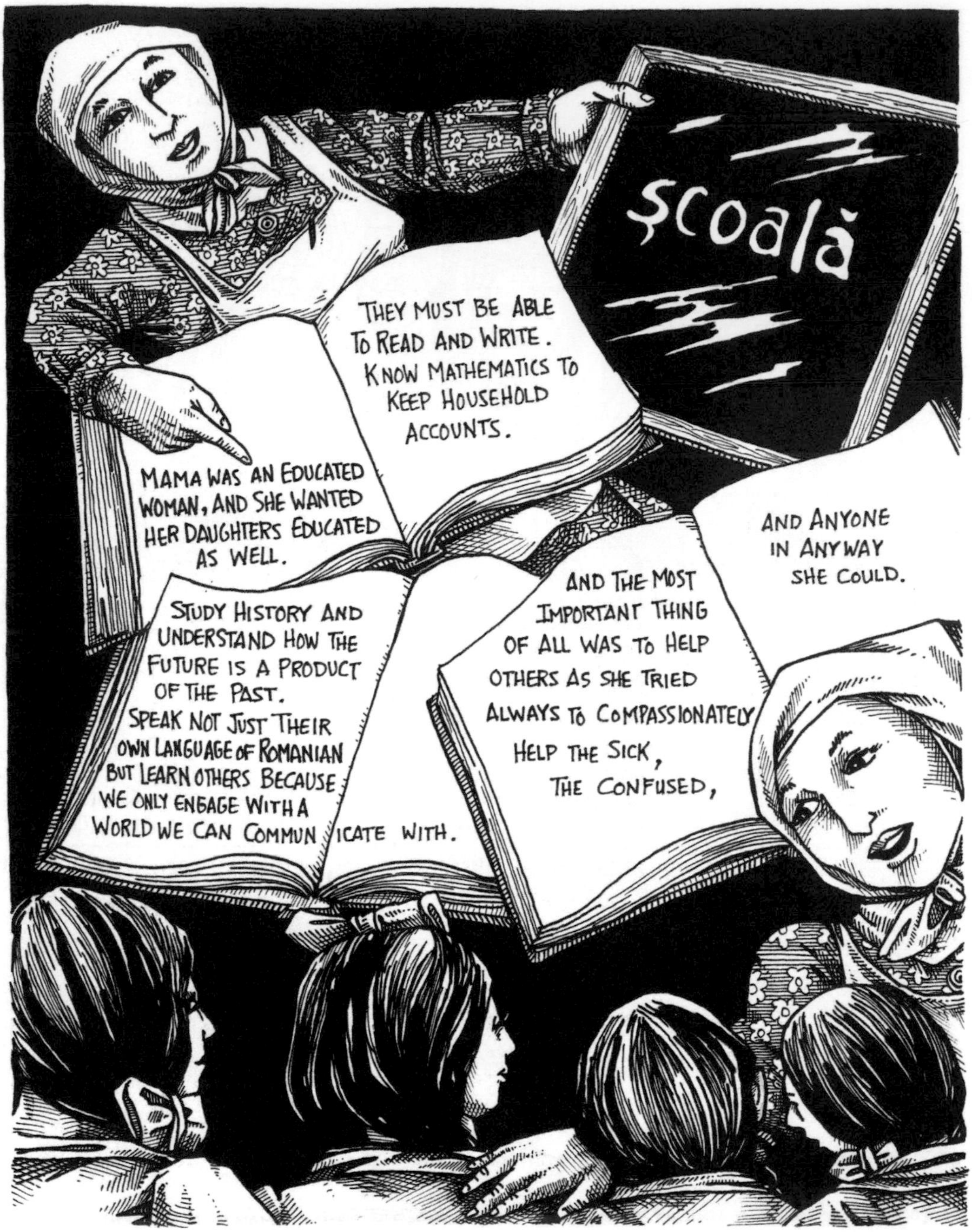
ȘCOALĂ
MAMA WAS AN EDUCATED WOMAN, AND SHE WANTED HER DAUGHTERS EDUCATED AS WELL.
THEY MUST BE ABLE TO READ AND WRITE. KNOW MATHEMATICS TO KEEP HOUSEHOLD ACCOUNTS.
STUDY HISTORY AND UNDERSTAND HOW THE FUTURE IS A PRODUCT OF THE PAST. SPEAK NOT JUST THEIR OWN LANGUAGE OF ROMANIAN BUT LEARN OTHERS BECAUSE WE ONLY ENGAGE WITH A WORLD WE CAN COMMUNICATE WITH.
AND THE MOST IMPORTANT THING OF ALL WAS TO HELP OTHERS AS SHE TRIED ALWAYS TO COMPASSIONATELY HELP THE SICK, THE CONFUSED,
AND ANYONE IN ANYWAY SHE COULD.

BUT AS STABLE AN ISLAND AS THE MOZES FAMILY STRIVED TO BE, THEY WERE SURROUNDED BY THE STORMY SEAS OF CHANGE. AND THESE CHANGES WERE NOT GOOD. THE IRON GUARD WAS A ROMANIAN POLITICAL PARTY WITH IDEAS VERY SIMILAR TO THOSE OF THE NAZIS TO THE NORTH. THEY GAINED POLITICAL CONTROL OF NORTHERN ROMANIA IN THE EARLY 1930s AND BEGAN THE CLEANSING OF THOSE THEY CONSIDERED NOT OF PURE ROMANIAN HERITAGE. JEWS WERE SEEN AS FOREIGN AND DANGEROUS TO ROMANIAN CHRISTIAN PURITY.

IN 1935, PAPA AND HIS BROTHER AARON WERE ARRESTED AND THROWN INTO PRISON ON FALSE CHARGES OF EVADING TAXES.

WHEN THEY WERE RELEASED, THE BROTHERS TRAVELED TO PALESTINE AND STAYED SEVERAL MONTHS TO INVESTIGATE THE POSSIBILITIES OF IMMIGRATION.

WHEN THEY RETURNED, PAPA INSISTED THAT THE FAMILY MOVE TO WHAT HAD HISTORICALLY BEEN THE JEWISH HOMELAND AS SOON AS THEY COULD.

NO! WE CAN'T GO.

MAMA ARGUED. HER PARENTS, THE HERSHES, WERE TOO OLD AND INFIRM TO MAKE THE JOURNEY, AND THEY COULD NOT SURVIVE WITHOUT MAMA'S CARE. THEY HAD A WONDERFUL FARM THAT WOULD SEE THEM THROUGH THESE TROUBLED TIMES AND THEY WOULD BE GOING TO A LAND WHERE THEY HAD NOTHING. IN ANY CASE, THE IRON GUARD AND THE NASTINESS HAPPENING AROUND THEM WAS ONLY A PHASE. THEY NEED NOT FEAR. MAMA'S ARGUMENT WON.

LIFE IN PORTZ CONTINUED WITH THE WORRIES OF THE REST OF THE WORLD ONLY A RUMOR TO BE AVOIDED.

THE TWINS PUT ON DRAMATIC PRODUCTIONS WITH THEIR BEST FRIEND, LUCI, THE LOCAL MINISTER'S DAUGHTER.

THEY RAN THROUGH THE FIELDS OF SUMMER. SCULPTED THE SNOWS OF WINTER AND HELPED DECORATE LUCI'S CHRISTMAS TREE. LAUGHED AND CRIED THE WAY CHILDREN DO.

EVEN WHEN JEWISH SLAVE LABOR FROM HUNGARY SOMETIMES CAME TO WORK ON THE RAILROAD AND STAYED IN THE FAMILY'S BARN, THE MOZES FAMILY FELT SAFE IN THE LITTLE VILLAGE.

BUT EVERYTHING CHANGED IN 1940. CHANGED WITH THE CHANGE IN GOVERNMENT AND HITLER ALLOWING FASCIST HUNGARY TO TAKE CONTROL OF NORTHERN ROMANIA. ANY ILLUSION OF SAFETY VANISHED.

AN OFFICER IN A SHINY BLACK CAR WITH TROOPS IN TOW BIVOUACKED IN THE MOZESES' FRONT YARD.

THE DASHING OFFICER KISSED MAMA'S HAND AND PATTED THE CHILDREN'S HEADS, BUT IT WASN'T REASSURING WITH SOLDIERS WITH THREATENING GUNS CAMPED UNDER THE KITCHEN WINDOW.

THE LOCAL TEACHERS WERE REPLACED WITH NEW HUNGARIAN TEACHERS. THE LESSONS CHANGED WITH THE STAFF. JEWS WERE CARICATURED AS MONEY-GRUBBING LEECHES, A DESTRUCTIVE FORCE IN SOCIETY, BENT ON NOTHING LESS THAN WORLD DOMINATION.

MOVIES WITH TITLES LIKE *HOW TO CATCH AND KILL A JEW* WERE INTRODUCED TO THE VILLAGE. THE TECHNOLOGY WAS CRUDE AND THE MESSAGES CRUDER AND FRIGHTENING. THE PEOPLE OF PORTZ WERE BEING INDOCTRINATED WITH HATE.

BULLYING STARTED. SHOUTS OF "DIRTY, SMELLY JEWS" FROM CLASSMATES AND FORMER FRIENDS MET THE MOZES CHILDREN AT EVERY CORNER.

SHOUTS BECAME ACTION. PUSHES, SHOVES, PUNCHES, AND SLAPS REPLACED GREETINGS.

WE MUST PRAY. WE MUST BE GOOD. THEY WILL COME TO THEIR SENSES.

EVA AND MIRIAM WERE TAKEN TO THE FRONT OF THE CLASSROOM. HARD KERNALS OF CORN WERE SPREAD ON THE WOODEN FLOOR. THEY WERE FORCED TO KNEEL FOR AN HOUR AND SUFFER THE TAUNTS OF THEIR CLASSMATES.

EVERY INCIDENT AT SCHOOL WAS BLAMED ON THE GIRLS. AS A PRANK, SOME EGGS WERE PUT ON A TEACHER'S CHAIR. IT HAD TO BE THE MOZES TWINS!

STILL EVA AND MIRIAM WENT TO SCHOOL.

THE FAMILY HIRED A JEWISH TUTOR FROM A NEIGHBORING TOWN TO WORK WITH EDIT AND ALIZ. EVENTUALLY THE TUTOR INSTRUCTED ALL THE GIRLS. HOME BECAME THE ONLY SAFE PLACE TO BE.

MORE AND MORE LOCAL BOYS JOINED THE HUNGARIAN NAZI PARTY. SOMETIMES AT NIGHT THEY WOULD SURROUND THE MOZES HOUSE SHOUTING SLURS AND THREATS OF VIOLENCE.

THEN IN JUNE 1941, HUNGARY ENTERED THE WAR AS AN AXIS POWER.

SHHHHH...

GET UP AND GET DRESSED IN YOUR WARMEST CLOTHES. PACK A SMALL BAG TO CARRY. WE ARE GOING SOUTH TO THE ROMANIA FREE OF HUNGARIAN CONTROL.

SEPTEMBER 1943. INTO THE COLD, WINDY NIGHT THE FAMILY FLED.

ALONG THE RAILROAD TRACKS. KEEPING TO THE SHADOWS IN THE FIELDS.

TO THE GATE AND FREEDOM?

HALT!

A VOICE COMMANDED FROM THE DARKNESS. SURROUNDED BY ARMED NAZI YOUTH, THEY WERE FORCED BACK TO THEIR HOME.

OCTOBER 1943. MAMA WAS SICK WITH TYPHOID. MONTHS WENT BY WITH MAMA STILL SICK SICK WITH AND PAPA WORRY.

THE DAYS BECAME ALL THE SAME. NO BIRTHDAY PARTIES OR ANY OTHER CELEBRATIONS. SCHOOL ONLY WHEN THE AUTHORITIES ALLOWED OR COMMANDED IT. A VIRTUAL HOUSE ARREST WITH FEAR GUARDING EVERY DOOR AND WINDOW.

MARCH 1944. TWO GENDARMES POUND ON THE DOOR.

YOU HAVE TWO HOURS TO PACK!

SILENCE.
THE VILLAGE LINED
THE MUDDY ROAD.

NO ONE SPOKE.
NOT EVEN LUCI, THE TWINS'
BEST FRIEND.
SOME TURNED THEIR BACKS.

THE MOZES FAMILY CLIMBED
ABOARD A HORSE-DRAWN WAGON
FOR THE FIVE-HOUR
TRIP TO THE
JEWISH GHETTO
OF ŞIMLEU
SILVANIEI.

THE GHETTO OF ŞIMLEU SILVANIEI WAS NOTHING BUT AN OPEN FIELD WITH AN ABANDONED BRICK FACTORY AND THE BERRETYO RIVER RUNNING THROUGH THE CENTER. THE FACTORY SERVED AS THE MILITARY HEADQUARTERS.

NO HOUSING AND NO TENTS WERE AVAILABLE FOR THE MORE THAN SEVEN THOUSAND INMATES OF THE CAMP. SHELTER WAS PATCHED TOGETHER WITH SHEETS, BLANKETS, TABLECLOTHS, ANYTHING LARGE ENOUGH TO COVER A SMALL PATCH OF GROUND.

PAPA LAUGHED. "LOOK, WE ARE LIKE THE CHILDREN OF ISRAEL IN THE DAYS OF MOSES."

BUT NO THIN COVERING COULD HELP MAMA'S SICKNESS. SHE SHIVERED AND GREW WEAKER.

PAPA WAS TAKEN BY THE GUARDS. THEIR FISTS AND KICKS TRIED TO COAX VALUABLES OUT OF HIM. ALL HE COULD OFFER WAS:

WE HAVE SILVER CANDLESTICKS FOR SHABBATS, AND THE ONLY OTHER THING OF VALUE IS OUR FARM.

THE MISERY OF THE
GHETTO CONTINUED
FOR WEEKS.

RAIN.

TWO WEEKS'
WORTH OF FOOD
THAT WAS QUICKLY,
EVEN WITH RATIONING
AND EDIT'S COOKING
SKILLS, GONE.

OCCASIONALLY, FOOD WAS TOSSED OVER THE FENCES
BY THE LOCAL PEOPLE, BUT NEVER ENOUGH.

MAMA IN THE THROES OF HER FEVER CRIED:

MY FAULT, ALL MY FAULT! IF ONLY WE
HAD GONE TO PALESTINE. IF ONLY...

THEN IT WAS MAY AND WORD CAME
THAT THE JEWS WERE BEING MOVED
TO LABOR CAMPS IN HUNGARY
AND NOT TO GERMANY
AND THE RUMORED
"DEATH CAMPS".

THE MOZES FAMILY ALONG WITH HUNDREDS OF OTHER PRISONERS WERE MARCHED TO THE TRAIN.

PAPA CARRIED HIS PRAYER BOOK. THE TWINS WERE DRESSED IN THEIR MATCHING BURGUNDY DRESSES, THE LAST BEAUTIFUL OUTFITS MAMA HAD MADE FOR THEM.

THE TRAIN WAS MADE UP OF CATTLE CARS.

EIGHTY TO ONE HUNDRED PEOPLE FORCED INTO EACH CAR.

NO ROOM TO LIE DOWN. NO ROOM TO SIT DOWN. NO TOILET. ONLY FOUR SMALL WINDOWS FOR VENTILATION.

THE TRAIN MOVED. FAST OR SLOW? NO ONE KNEW ANYTHING OTHER THAN IT MOVED.

AT THE FIRST STOP, HAVING TRAVELED FOR HOURS WITHOUT PROVISIONS, THE INMATES PLEADED FOR WATER.

WATER.

WATER.

WATER.

WATER? SURE. WHAT CAN YOU PAY?

FIVE GOLD WATCHES WERE OFFERED UP.

A BUCKET OF DIRTY WATER WAS SLOSHED THROUGH ONE OF THE WINDOWS.

THE PEOPLE ACHED FOR DROPS.   THE TRAIN MOVED AGAIN.

HOURS MORE ON THE JOLTING TRAIN.

FOOD? WATER? PLEASE?

THE CRIES WENT UNANSWERED.

SLEEP WAS IMPOSSIBLE, ONLY A KIND OF SICK TRANCE JOSTLING INTO THE SHOULDERS AND KNEES OF THE PEOPLE WHO SURROUNDED.

AND THE TRAIN MOVED ON.

HOPE WAS REPLACED BY FEAR.

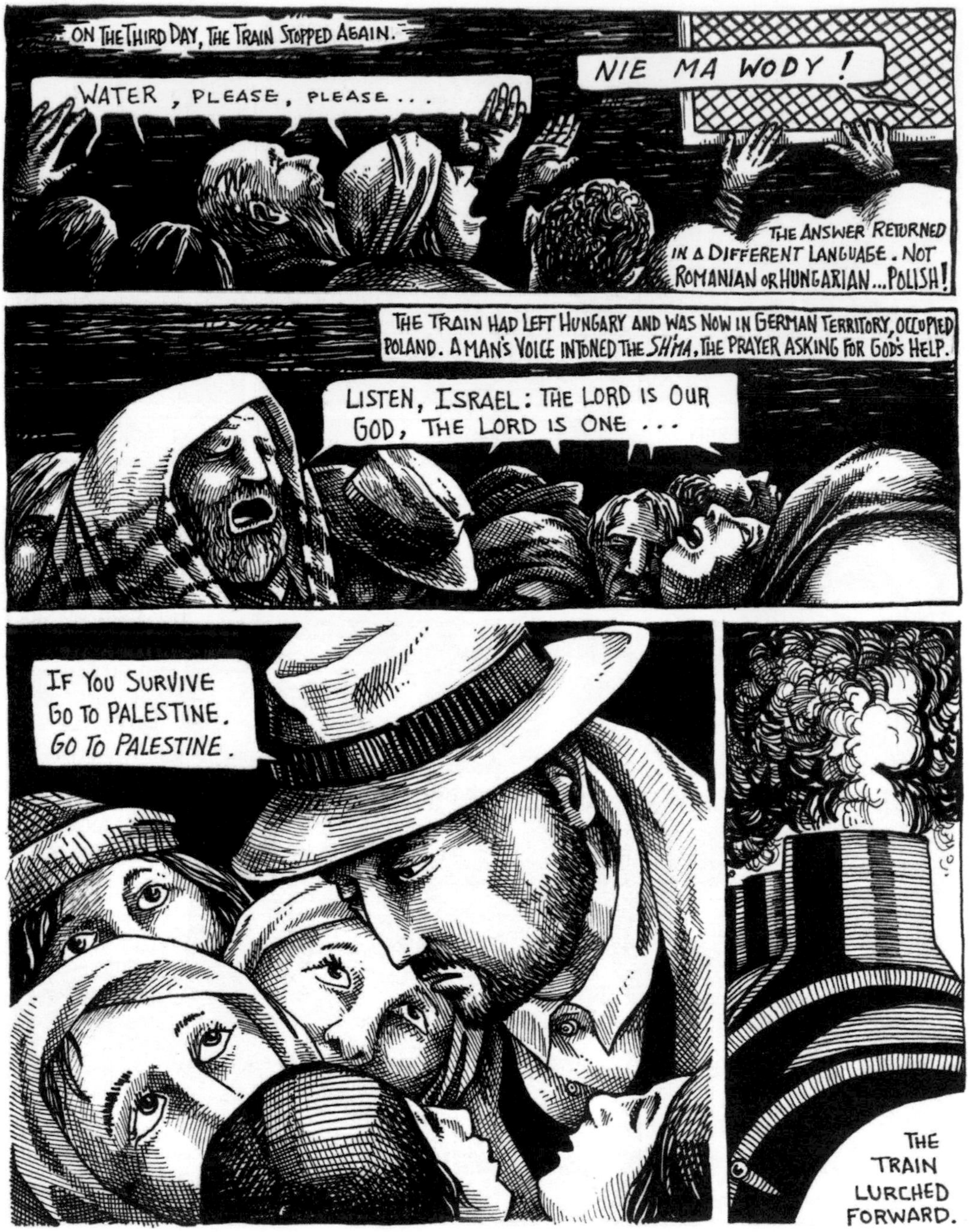
ON THE THIRD DAY, THE TRAIN STOPPED AGAIN.
WATER, PLEASE, PLEASE...
NIE MA WODY!
THE ANSWER RETURNED IN A DIFFERENT LANGUAGE. NOT ROMANIAN OR HUNGARIAN... POLISH!
THE TRAIN HAD LEFT HUNGARY AND WAS NOW IN GERMAN TERRITORY, OCCUPIED POLAND. A MAN'S VOICE INTONED THE SH'MA, THE PRAYER ASKING FOR GOD'S HELP.
LISTEN, ISRAEL: THE LORD IS OUR GOD, THE LORD IS ONE...
IF YOU SURVIVE GO TO PALESTINE. GO TO PALESTINE.
THE TRAIN LURCHED FORWARD.

THE FOURTH DAY. THE TRAIN SLOWED. AND SLOWED. STOPPED.

ACHTUNG! ROUS! RUS! BARK! BARK!

DOGS WERE BARKING. VOICES SHOUTED. THE DOOR OF THE CATTLE CAR SCREECHED OPEN ONTO...

THE SELECTION PLATFORM OF AUSCHWITZ-BIRKENAU — THE NAZIS' LARGEST DEATH CAMP.

CHAPTER 3: AUSCHWITZ-BIRKENAU

SCREAMING, SHOUTING, CRYING, DOGS BARKING—DEAFENING NOISE! THE SICK SMELL OF BURNING FEATHERS, BURNING MEAT. PEOPLE CAME OFF THE TRAIN WHILE SS GUARDS PUSHED AND BEAT THEM INTO LINES.

DOCTORS IN WHITE COATS DIRECTED INTO WHICH LINES THEY WERE TO BE PUT. THE MOZESES STRUGGLED TO STAY TOGETHER.

IN A BREATH, PAPA, EDIT, AND ALIZ WERE GONE.
MAMA CLUNG TO EVA AND MIRIAM.

ZWILLINGE?

ZWILLINGE? TWINS? IS THAT GOOD?

THE GUARD TOOK THE GIRLS. MAMA WAS PULLED AWAY IN THE OTHER DIRECTION, SCREAMING FOR HER BABIES.

YES, THEY ARE TWINS.

JA! YES!

AUSCHWITZ-BIRKENAU, WHAT WAS THIS PLACE? AUSCHWITZ I WAS ORIGINALLY A POLISH MILITARY CAMP BUILT OUTSIDE THE TOWN OF OŚWIĘCIM.

IN 1940, THE NAZIS STARTED USING THE BRICK BARRACKS AS A TRANSIT CAMP FOR POLISH POLITICAL PRISONERS.

SOON THE CAMP EXPANDED TO IMPRISON SOVIET POWs AND OTHER TYPES OF INMATES DISTINGUISHABLE BY THE TRIANGLE BADGES SEWN ON THE LEFT BREAST OF THEIR BLUE AND GRAY STRIPED UNIFORMS. BY 1941, AUSCHWITZ I (WHICH HELD OVER EIGHTEEN THOUSAND AT ITS PEAK) WAS NO LONGER ABLE TO HANDLE THE INCREASING NUMBER OF PRISONERS.

CONSTRUCTION ON AUSCHWITZ II-BIRKENAU WAS BEGUN A SHORT DISTANCE AWAY AFTER THE INHABITANTS OF THE VILLAGE OF BRZEZINKA WERE EXPELLED AND THE BUILDINGS DESTROYED.

BIRKENAU WAS PRIMARILY WOODEN BARRACKS (THE FIRST OF THESE WERE INTENDED AS STABLES) WITH TWENTY OR SO BRICK AND STONE STRUCTURES. OVER THREE HUNDRED BUILDINGS WERE EVENTUALLY BUILT TO HOUSE UP TO ONE HUNDRED THOUSAND INNOCENT PEOPLE.

IN 1942 AFTER THE WANNSEE CONFERENCE AND THE DECISION TO MURDER ALL OF EUROPEAN JEWRY, BIRKENAU BECAME THE NAZIS' LARGEST DEATH CAMP. FOUR GAS CHAMBERS WITH CREMATORIUMS WERE BUILT TO CARRY OUT THE MASS EXECUTIONS.

THE MOZES FAMILY ARRIVED IN MARCH 1944 WHEN SELECTIONS WERE BEING DONE ON THE RAILROAD PLATFORM IN THE CENTER OF BIRKENAU.

MOST OF THE PEOPLE COMING OUT OF THE TRAINS WERE SELECTED FOR IMMEDIATE DEATH IN THE GAS CHAMBERS (THEY WERE TOLD THEY WERE GOING TO THE SHOWERS) TWIN CHILDREN WERE CONSIDERED SPECIAL.

THE TWINS WERE TAKEN TO STAND WITH A GROUP OF CHILDREN. AMONG THEM STOOD MRS. CSENGERI WITH HER EIGHT-YEAR-OLD TWINS THAT THEY HAD GOTTEN TO KNOW IN ŞIMLEU SILVANIEI. A FINGER TO MRS. CSENGERI'S LIPS BROUGHT AN ANXIOUS SILENCE.

THE CHILDREN WERE MARCHED TO A BIG BUILDING NEAR THE FENCE.

THEY WERE FORCED TO UNDRESS.

THEIR LONG BRAIDS WERE CHOPPED OFF AND TOSSED INTO A GROWING PILE OF HAIR.

AFTER SHOWERS, THEIR FUMIGATED CLOTHES WERE RETURNED WITH A RED CROSS PAINTED ON THE BACK.

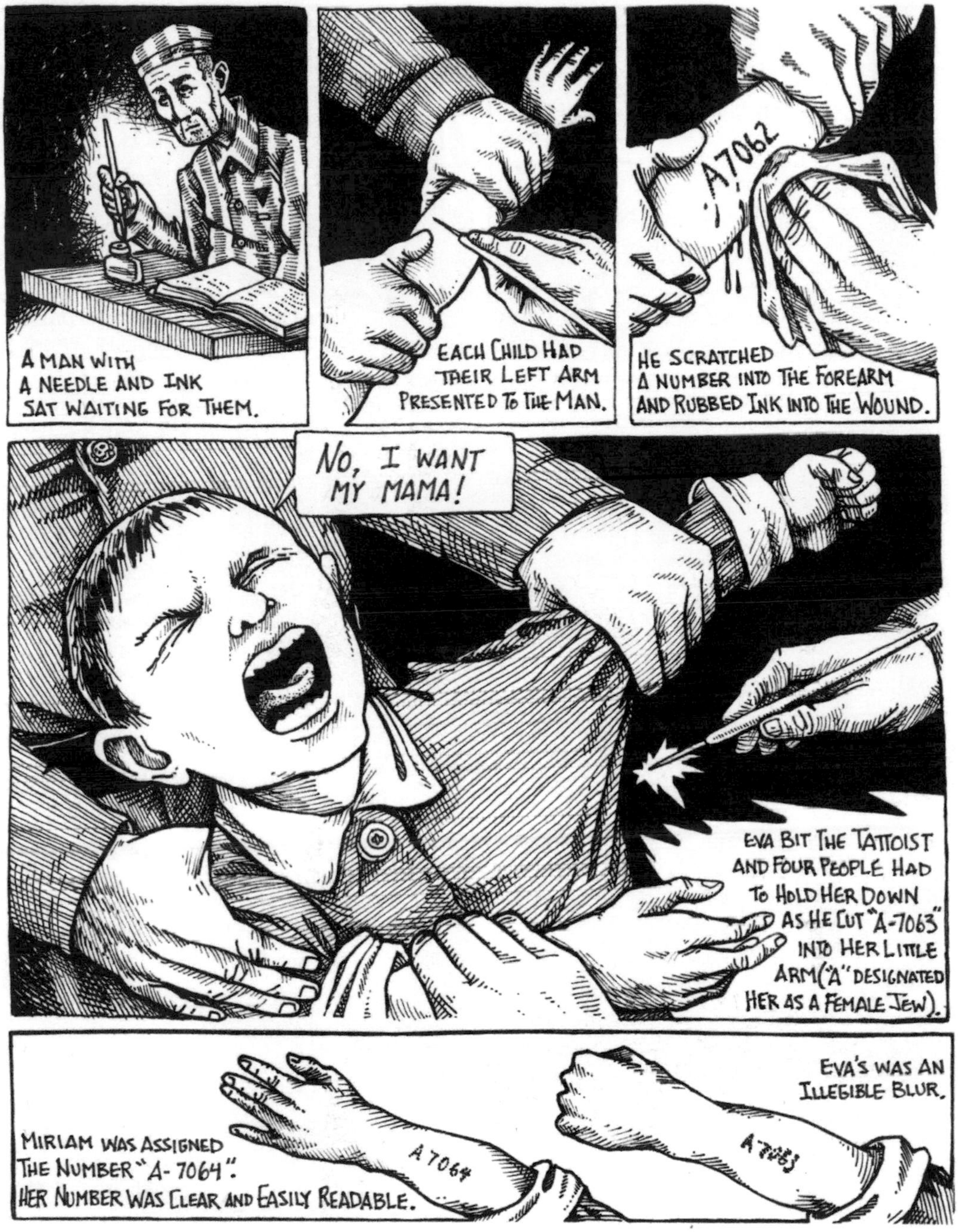
A MAN WITH A NEEDLE AND INK SAT WAITING FOR THEM.
EACH CHILD HAD THEIR LEFT ARM PRESENTED TO THE MAN.
A7062
HE SCRATCHED A NUMBER INTO THE FOREARM AND RUBBED INK INTO THE WOUND.
NO, I WANT MY MAMA!
EVA BIT THE TATTOIST AND FOUR PEOPLE HAD TO HOLD HER DOWN AS HE CUT "A-7063" INTO HER LITTLE ARM ("A" DESIGNATED HER AS A FEMALE JEW).
MIRIAM WAS ASSIGNED THE NUMBER "A-7064". HER NUMBER WAS CLEAR AND EASILY READABLE.
A 7064
EVA'S WAS AN ILLEGIBLE BLUR.

THE CHILDREN WERE SEPARATED INTO BOYS AND GIRLS AND LED THROUGH THE CAMP TO THEIR BARRACKS.
SLAVE-LABORERS WERE RETURNING TO THE CAMP WITH SS GUARDS AND SNARLING DOGS FORCING THEM TO "MACHT SCHNELL" (MAKE FASTER).

SOME OF THE PRISONERS WERE LITTLE MORE THAN SKELETONS, THE MUSSELMANNER. WORK, DEPRIVATION, AND TORTURE HAD REDUCED THEM TO THIN SHADOWS.

FINALLY, CAMP II, THE GIRLS' CAMP. THEIR QUARTERS, A FORMER STABLE WITH A DOUBLE ROW OF BRICKS FORMING A BENCH DOWN THE CENTER, TRIPLE-DECKER BUNKS, ABOVE A LINE OF WINDOWS ALLOWING A DIM LIGHT, AND ONE OF THE FEW BARRACKS WITH A THREE-HOLE LATRINE.

EVA AND MIRIAM WERE ASSIGNED A BED ON THE BOTTOM TIER.

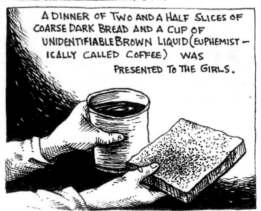

A DINNER OF TWO AND A HALF SLICES OF COARSE DARK BREAD AND A CUP OF UNIDENTIFIABLE BROWN LIQUID (EUPHEMISTICALLY CALLED COFFEE) WAS PRESENTED TO THE GIRLS.

UGH! WE CAN'T EAT THIS. IT ISN'T KOSHER.

THEN YOU ARE HUNGRY UNTIL TOMORROW. EAT OR STARVE. THIS IS BIRKENAU, A DEATH CAMP! IF YOU ARE YOUNG AND STRONG, THEY SAVE YOU TO WORK TO DEATH. IF YOU ARE NOT YOUNG AND STRONG, YOU GO STRAIGHT TO THE GAS CHAMBER AND UP THE CHIMNEY.

WHAT DO YOU THINK THE SMOKE AND STINK IS? WE ARE ONLY ALIVE BECAUSE DR. MENGELE EXPERIMENTS ON US. HE LIKES TWINS.

EVA AND MIRIAM HUDDLED TOGETHER ON THE THIN MATTRESS. THEIR WORLD HAD BEEN COMPLETELY OVERTURNED, STOLEN AWAY, AND REPLACED WITH A NIGHTMARE.

WHERE WERE MAMA AND PAPA, EDIT AND ALIZ? WHAT WAS GOING TO HAPPEN NEXT?

43

TOSSING, TURNING, THE BITES OF LICE AND FLEAS IN THE BED, THE NIGHT WAS MISERABLE. STRANGE SCUFFLING SOUNDS FROM UNDER THE BED. EVA PEERED OVER THE EDGE.

MICE!

NO, NOT MICE. RATS. THEY WON'T BOTHER YOU AS LONG AS YOU DON'T HAVE FOOD IN YOUR BED.

SLEEP IMPOSSIBLE, THE TWINS SCRAMBLED RATS AWAY AS THEY WENT TO THE LATRINE.

NO! THERE ON THE FLOOR WERE THREE DEAD, NAKED CHILDREN. TRANSFIXED WITH THE HORROR THEIR LIVES HAD BECOME...

EVA VOWED NOT TO BECOME ONE OF THOSE CHILDREN. SHE WOULD DO EVERYTHING FOR HER AND MIRIAM TO SURVIVE.

THE MORNING WHISTLE! A NURSE SHOUTED, "READY!"

ALL THE GIRLS FILED OUT AND ASSEMBLED INTO FIVE ROWS. THEY STOOD FOR OVER AN HOUR AND A HALF FOR THE ROLL CALL. THEN RETURNED TO THE BARRACKS TO CLEAN IT.

AN SS GUARD BURST INTO THE BARRACKS. "DR. MENGELE IS COMING!"

THE HANDSOME DR. MENGELE ARRIVED IN HIS CRISP SS UNIFORM SURROUNDED BY AN ENTOURAGE OF EIGHT.

"HOW COULD YOU LET THREE CHILDREN DIE? NEVER LET THIS HAPPEN AGAIN!"

DR. JOSEF MENGELE WAS A PHYSICIAN ASSIGNED TO AUSCHWITZ-BIRKENAU TO CARRY OUT RESEARCH AND EXPERIMENTS. HIS MAIN INTERESTS CENTERED ON STRENGTHENING THE NUMBERS OF THE ARYAN RACE AND LIMITING THE BIRTHS OF RACES NAZIS DEEMED INFERIOR. HE WAS PARTICULARLY FASCINATED BY TWINS AND CREATING MULTIPLE OFFSPRING. THE INJECTIONS OF CHEMICALS AND BIZARRE SUBSTANCES, AMPUTATIONS, AND OTHER TORTURES HE DEVISED IN HIS LABORATORY UNDER THE GUISE OF SCIENCE TO CHILDREN AND OTHER UNFORTUNATES (DWARFS, GIANTS, ROMA, AND THE DISABLED) REMAIN SOME OF AUSCHWITZ'S MOST HORRIBLE ATROCITIES. THEY ALONG WITH HIS COMMAND OF THE SELECTION PROCESS SENDING THOSE TO THE RIGHT IMMEDIATELY TO THE GAS CHAMBERS AND THOSE TO THE LEFT TO LABOR AND EVENTUAL DEATH EARNED HIM THE NICKNAME THE ANGEL OF DEATH.

AFTER *COFFEE* THE GIRLS WERE MARCHED FROM BIRKENAU TO THE TWO-STORY BRICK LABORATORY IN AUSCHWITZ I.

THEY WERE FORCED TO STRIP NAKED IN THE COMPANY OF THE BOYS WHO HAD ALSO ARRIVED AND THE EXAMINATIONS BEGAN.

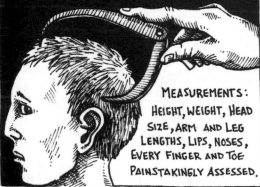

MEASUREMENTS: HEIGHT, WEIGHT, HEAD SIZE, ARM AND LEG LENGTHS, LIPS, NOSES, EVERY FINGER AND TOE PAINSTAKINGLY ASSESSED.

EYE COLOR WAS OF PARTICULAR INTEREST TO MENGELE. HE WANTED TO UNLOCK THE SECRET OF BLUE EYES IN HOPES OF GENETICALLY ENCOURAGING THAT MOST ARYAN OF COLORS.

PHOTOS, SKETCHES, X-RAYS, EVERY INCH OF THE CHILDREN'S BODIES WERE CATALOGED ALONG WITH SOME PSYCHOLOGICAL TESTING TO DETERMINE THE VARIABLES OF EACH PERSONALITY.

EVA, EVER THE TROUBLEMAKER, ARGUED ABOUT THE HUMILIATION AND DISCOMFORT OF ENDLESS EXAMINATION. HER LEADERSHIP WAS DULY NOTED IN HER CHARTS.

THE LONG DAY ENDED WITH A MARCH BACK TO THE BARRACKS IN BIRKENAU UNDER THE COMMAND OF THE NURSE.

UNLIKE THE BOYS WHO LIVED WITH ZVI SPIEGEL, AN ADULT IN CHARGE OF THEIR BARRACKS, WHO ENGAGED, TAUGHT, COMFORTED, AND AS MUCH AS HE WAS ABLE, PROTECTED THEM, THE GIRLS' NURSE WAS A WOMAN THEY CALLED SNAKE.

SNAKE HAD NO RESPECT OR LIKING FOR HER CHARGES. SHE ABUSED THEM WITH TAUNTS, INSULTS, AND THE PHYSICAL VIOLENCE SHE METED OUT WITH HER THICK ARMS AND LEGS.

HER NICKNAME DERIVED NOT JUST FROM HER VENOMOUS ATTITUDE BUT ALSO FROM THE LONG SINGLE BRAID THAT HUNG DOWN HER BACK.

SOMETIMES SNAKE FORCED THE GIRLS TO DO A CIRCLE DANCE, SINGING:* "I AM A LITTLE GERMAN CHILD AND IF I'M NOT, PHOOEY, PHOOEY, PHOOEY!"

HA, THE ONLY REASON YOU ARE ALIVE IS FOR DR. MENGELE TO EXPERIMENT ON, AND WHEN HE'S DONE, YOU ARE OFF TO THE GAS CHAMBER AND UP THE CHIMNEY!

THE TORTURE AND TEARS OF THE FIRST DAYS CALLOUSED INTO NUMBNESS. THREE TIMES A WEEK TO THE LAB IN AUSCHWITZ. MEASUREMENTS, INJECTIONS, AND SOME CHILDREN SUBJECTED TO BIZARRE SURGERIES, SURGERIES THAT MUTILATED, DISABLED, AND OFTEN KILLED THE YOUNG PEOPLE FORCED TO UNDERGO THEM, AND IF ONE TWIN DIED DURING A PROCEDURE THE OTHER TWIN WAS EXECUTED.

THREE DAYS A WEEK TO THE BLOOD LAB IN BIRKENAU AND THE ENDLESS DRAWING OF BLOOD AND MORE AND MORE INJECTIONS OF UNKNOWN SUBSTANCES, DISEASES, BACTERIA, CHEMICALS, POISONS, ONLY THE NAZI DOCTORS AND NURSES KNEW WHAT WAS BEING FORCED INTO THE CHILDREN'S BODIES.

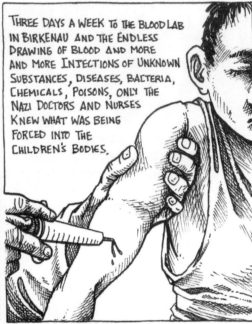

ONCE A WEEK TO TAKE A SHOWER, AND WHILE SHOWERING, CLOTHES WOULD BE DISINFECTED WITH **ZYKLON B**, THE SAME PESTICIDE CRYSTALS THAT WERE USED IN THE GAS CHAMBERS.

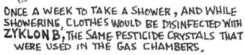

THE BARRACKS WERE CLEANED WHILE THE GIRLS WERE AWAY. MENGELE'S EXPERIMENTS MUST NOT BE CONTAMINATED, BUT THE LICE, FLEAS, AND RATS ALWAYS CAME BACK.

LIFE CONTINUED IN ITS WAY...
THE OLDER GIRLS TRIED
TO PLAY WITH AND NOURISH
THE YOUNGER.

WHEN DRESSES WORE OUT THEY WERE REPLACED WITH
THE GARMENTS OF OLDER WOMEN, MUCH TOO BIG,
BUT BOUND WITH ROPE THEY COULD HOLD A
CUP, A BIT OF BREAD, WHATEVER BITS
AND PIECES ONE COULD
COME BY.

AN OLDER GIRL TAUGHT EVA AND MIRIAM TO KNIT
USING NEEDLES STRAIGHTENED FROM SCRAPS OF
FENCE AND A RAG OF SWEATER PAINSTAKINGLY
UNRAVELED.

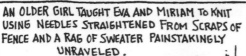

MRS. CSENGERI, WHO HAD SURVIVED BY CONVINCING
DR. MENGELE THAT SHE COULD PROVIDE HIM WITH IMPORT-
ANT INFORMATION, SOMETIMES WOULD SNEAK IN TO
CHECK ON HER DAUGHTERS AND THE MOZES TWINS.

BUT THE OCCASIONAL VISIT OF A CARING ADULT AND THE ACCOMPLISHMENT OF A NEW SKILL LEARNED
COULD NOT TAKE AWAY THE CONSTANCY OF DEATH.

MY MAMA!...

IN JULY, THE TWINS WERE INJECTED WITH DISEASE.

THAT NIGHT THEY THRASHED WITH FEVER, HEADACHES, BURNING SKIN, AND UNCONTROLLABLE SHAKING.

BY ROLL CALL, THE SYMPTOMS INCLUDED SWOLLEN ARMS AND LEGS AND RED PATCHES OF PAINFUL RASH, BUT SNAKE MUST NEVER KNOW BECAUSE CHILDREN LIVED WITH THE LAW, TWICE SICK AND YOU NEVER RETURN.

EVEN IN THE MIDST OF TERRIBLE SICKNESS IN THIS HELLISH PLACE, HOPE STILL FOUND ITS HOME.

AN AIR RAID SIREN SCREAMED AND THE SS GUARDS SCURRIED FOR COVER BECAUSE AN AMERICAN PLANE CIRCLED THE CAMP, LEAVING NOTHING MORE DESTRUCTIVE THAN A CIRCLE OF YELLOW SMOKE. THE JOY OF SEEING THEIR OPPRESSORS RUN AND HIDE RAISED CHEERS AND THE SENSE THE NAZIS WERE NOT INVINCIBLE. THIS COULD END!

THE ROUTINE WAS BROKEN WHEN THE BLOOD LAB NURSES REALIZED EVA HAD A CONTINUING FEVER.

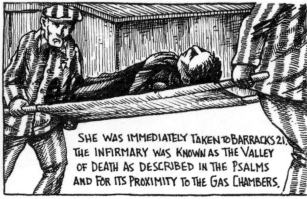

SHE WAS IMMEDIATELY TAKEN TO BARRACKS 21. THE INFIRMARY WAS KNOWN AS THE VALLEY OF DEATH AS DESCRIBED IN THE PSALMS AND FOR ITS PROXIMITY TO THE GAS CHAMBERS.

NO FOOD RATION WAS GIVEN PATIENTS AS THEY WERE CONSIDERED TERMINAL AND THEIR SYMPHONY OF SUFFERING CHORUSED THROUGH THE LONG HOURS.

TWICE A WEEK TRUCKS CAME TO TAKE THE SICKEST AWAY TO BE EXECUTED.

DR. MENGELE CHUCKLED WHEN HE EXAMINED EVA.

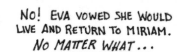

TOO BAD. SO YOUNG AND ONLY TWO WEEKS TO LIVE.

NO! EVA VOWED SHE WOULD LIVE AND RETURN TO MIRIAM. *NO MATTER WHAT...*

STILL BURNING WITH FEVER, EVA WAS THIRSTY, BUT NO WATER WAS OFFERED.

SHE HAD SEEN A FAUCET AT THE END OF THE BARRACKS.

EACH NIGHT, SHE GOT OUT OF HER BED, AND BEING TOO WEAK TO WALK, SHE CRAWLED INCH BY INCH ACROSS THE FILTHY CONCRETE. EVERY NIGHT FOR TWO WEEKS, SHE CRAWLED TO TAKE HER LIFESAVING DRINK.

MRS. CSENGERI PROVED TO BE NOT JUST A GIVER OF HOPE BUT ALSO OF BREAD. MIRIAM SAVED HER SMALL PORTION FOR THOSE WEEKS, AND MRS. CSENGERI WOULD SNEAK IT TO EVA.

ONCE SHE BROUGHT CAKE TO EVA AND HER STARVING BEDMATES, TWINS VERA AND TAMARA WITH CHICKEN POX.

DR. MENGELE CAME INTO THE INFIRMARY TWICE A DAY TO CHECK ON HIS PRECIOUS TWINS. IF ONE DIED, MENGELE WOULD KILL THE SURVIVING TWIN WITH A SHOT OF CHLOROFORM OR PHENOL INTO THE HEART. THE BODIES WERE TAKEN TO DR. MIKLÓS NYISZLI, A JEWISH PATHOLOGIST FORCED INTO SERVICE, FOR AN AUTOPSY. THE INFORMATION WAS THEN SENT TO THE ANTHROPOLOGICAL INSTITUTE IN BERLIN.

EVA DECIDED SHE HAD TO LOWER HER TEMPERATURE : SHE WOULD TAKE THE THERMOMETER OUT FROM UNDER HER ARMPIT AND SHAKE IT DOWN WHILE NO ONE WAS LOOKING.

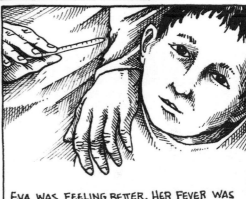

EVA WAS FEELING BETTER. HER FEVER WAS BREAKING. SHE HAD TO GET BACK TO MIRIAM.

AT LAST, EVA WAS SENT BACK TO THE GIRLS' CAMP.

MIRIAM HAD BECOME A *MUSSELMANN*! ONE OF THE WALKING DEAD! SHE, LISTLESS, LIFELESS, HAD STOPPED EATING AND WAS BARELY BREATHING.

DURING THE WEEKS EVA HAD BEEN GONE, THE EXPERIMENTS ON MIRIAM HAD CONTINUED. INJECTION AFTER INJECTION OF ONLY WHAT THE NAZI DOCTORS KNEW.

EVERYONE IN CAMP HAD DYSENTERY, SO EVA KNEW IT WAS MORE THAN THAT, AND EVA KNEW THAT ONE THING SHE COULD DO WAS FEED HER SISTER MORE THAN THE MEAGER CAMP RATIONS.

EVA WOULD "ORGANIZE" – THE CAMP SLANG FOR STEALING – MORE FOOD. STEALING WAS DANGEROUS. ANYONE CAUGHT DOING IT WOULD BE HANGED ALONG WITH THOSE CAUGHT TRYING TO ESCAPE OR ANY OTHER INFRACTION OF THE CAMP RULES. CHILDREN WERE HANGED THE SAME AS ADULTS. A GIBBET WAS PERMANENTLY ERECTED IN FRONT OF BLOCK 11 FOR THE PURPOSE

EVA HAD ONLY STOLEN ONCE. SHE HAD TAKEN A TIN CUP FROM A PILE OF CONFISCATED POTS AND PANS. AND SHE HAD GOTTEN AWAY WITH IT.

EVA VOLUNTEERED TO BE A FOOD CARRIER. THIS WOULD GET HER INTO THE KITCHEN.

THE SECOND TIME EVA VOLUNTEERED, SHE GOT THE JOB. SHE AND ANOTHER GIRL WERE MARCHED TO THE KITCHEN.

A LONG METAL TABLE WAS STACKED WITH POTS AND PANS. TWO LARGE SACKS OF POTATOES WERE NEARBY. A THIRTY-GALLON VAT OF WATERY SOUP WITH A FEW CLUMPS OF POTATO WAITED TO BE CARRIED BACK TO THE BARRACKS.

EVA LOOKED AROUND. NO ONE SEEMED TO BE PAYING ATTENTION. SHE REACHED INTO THE NEAREST SACK AND TOOK TWO POTATOES.

A HAND CLAMPED DOWN ON HER SHOULDER. "YOU CAN'T DO THAT!"

DO WHAT, MADAME?

STEAL POTATOES! NOW PUT THEM BACK.

EVA PUT THEM BACK AND WAITED...

EVA WAS NOT TAKEN TO BE HANGED. AS ONE OF MENGELE'S EXPERIMENTS, SHE WAS TO BE KEPT ALIVE AT HIS DISCRETION. BACK AT THE BARRACKS, SHE STILL FEARED THE WRATH OF SNAKE AND THE BLOCOVA, THE BLOCK SUPERVISOR, BUT NOTHING WAS SAID.

SHE VOLUNTEERED AS FOOD CARRIER AGAIN AND WAS CHOSEN. SUCCESS! EVA SLIPPED THREE POTATOES INTO THE FOLDS OF HER DRESS.

THE POTATOES WERE BOILED, DIRT AND ALL, ON THE BRICK STOVE AT THE FRONT OF THE BARRACKS HEATED WITH ORGANIZED COAL AFTER THE BLOCOVA HAD GONE TO BED. THE GIRLS WHO HAD MANAGED TO SECURE A FEW EXTRA MORSELS TOOK TURNS BEING LOOKOUT WHILE THEY HEATED THEIR ORGANIZED FOOD. THEY TAPPED THEIR FEET AS AN ALERT. AND NO ONE EVER TOOK OR REPORTED THE LIFESAVING FOOD.

AND LIFESAVING IT WAS. MIRIAM WAS RETURNED TO LIFE AS EVA WAS ABLE TO EVADE CAPTURE AND WAS ABLE TO ORGANIZE POTATOES TWO OR THREE TIMES A WEEK. AS EVA WOULD *LATER* SAY:

DYING IN AUSCHWITZ WAS EASY; SURVIVING WAS A FULL-TIME JOB.

In Autumn of 1944, bombing came closer and closer. The war was finally coming to the camp.

During the night of October 7, an explosion rocked the camp. Sirens blared! The Sonderkommandos (able-bodied Jewish men who had been conscripted to do the things the SS didn't want to do; take the dead bodies from the gas chamber, pull gold teeth, cut the women's hair...) had revolted.

They blew up Krema 4 with smuggled explosives. But the courageous act of rebellion was met with quick retaliation, and the Sonderkommandos who had taken part were summarily executed.

Then, the entire Roma camp was taken to the gas chambers, and two thousand or more men, women, and children were murdered seemingly overnight. They left the walls of their barracks covered with murals and left all the small possessions, including blankets, they had gathered.

The children were moved into the empty barracks. Even closer to the smoking Kremas.

LIFE CONTINUED THE SAME AS IT HAD, BUT FEAR AND TENSION WERE GROWING.

SOMEONE WAS MISSING FROM THE MORNING ROLL CALL. THE CAMP STOOD AT ATTENTION FROM 5:00 IN THE MORNING UNTIL 4:00 IN THE AFTERNOON. THE ESCAPEE WAS NEVER FOUND.

RAUS! RAUS!

EVERYONE IN THE CAMP WAS COMMANDED OUT OF THEIR BARRACKS. ALL THE ABLE-BODIED WERE TO EVACUATE THE CAMP. ABOUT FIFTY-SIX THOUSAND PRISONERS WERE ORDERED TO MARCH FROM POLAND TO GERMANY IN THE FREEZING COLD OF MID-JANUARY.

EVA AND MIRIAM HID IN THEIR BARRACKS.

THE CAMP WAS VIRTUALLY EMPTY! MRS. CSENGERI AND HER TWINS HAD MANAGED TO STAY AS WELL AS SOME OF THE OTHER CHILDREN AND PRISONERS. BUT THE SS, THE NAZIS WERE GONE.

THEY DISCOVERED A HOLE IN THE FENCE AND MADE THEIR WAY TO KANADA (KANADA WAS NAMED FOR THE COUNTRY IN NORTH AMERICA THAT WAS FABLED TO BE A LAND OF RICHES), THE BUILDING PILED WITH THE CLOTHING AND POSSESSIONS TAKEN FROM EVERYONE AS THEY CAME INTO THE CAMP.

DRESSES, COATS, HATS, BLANKETS, SHOES! ALMOST EVERYTHING WAS TOO BIG, BUT LAYERS COULD HELP A FIT. RAGS TIED AROUND FEET COULD MAKE A PAIR OF SHOES WORK, ESPECIALLY AFTER THE PAIR EVA HAD ARRIVED IN WERE TORN AND FLAPPING AFTER MONTHS OF ABUSE.

EVA LEFT MIRIAM TO GUARD THEIR NEW ACQUISITIONS AND MADE HER WAY TO ORGANIZE FOOD.

59

IN THE KITCHEN, EVA FOUND LOAVES OF BREAD. ALL SHE COULD CARRY.

SHE EXITED THE KITCHEN WITH THE OTHER SCAVENGERS AND WAS MAKING HER WAY BACK TO THE BARRACKS WHEN VEHICLES SLID TO A STOP IN FRONT OF THEM. THE NAZIS WERE BACK!

THEY STARTED FIRING ON THE CROWD OF STARVING INMATES. BODIES FELL AROUND EVA.

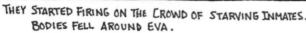

AN SS MAN POINTED HIS RIFLE AT EVA'S HEAD.

SHE FAINTED.

EVA WOKE UP SURROUNDED BY BODIES.

CAREFULLY SHE MADE HER WAY BACK TO THE BARRACKS.

MIRIAM! THE NAZIS ARE BACK! I COULDN'T GET BREAD.

EVA, WHAT IF...?

FIRE AND EXPLOSIONS EVERYWHERE. THE GAS CHAMBERS AND CREMATORIUMS WERE BLOWN UP. KANADA I WAS BURNING. THE NAZIS WERE DESTROYING EVIDENCE.

THE ALLIES WERE BOMBING ALL AROUND. THE WORLD WAS ON FIRE!

ALL THE REMAINING PRISONERS WERE PULLED OUT OF THE BARRACKS AND LINED UP.

THE SS SHOT PEOPLE AT RANDOM. EVA AND MIRIAM SQUEEZED INTO THE MIDDLE OF THE CROWD.

SOME EIGHTY-TWO HUNDRED INMATES WERE MARCHED FROM BIRKENAU TO AUSCHWITZ I.

AROUND TWELVE HUNDRED WERE SHOT AND KILLED IN THE HOUR IT TOOK TO WALK THE SHORT DISTANCE.

LIGHTS WERE GLOWING THROUGH OUT THE CAMP. THE TERRIFIED PRISONERS RAN FOR THE COVER OF THE BRICK BUILDINGS. BUT THE SS GUARDS MYSTERIOUSLY VANISHED. IN THE TERRIBLE CONFUSION, EVA LOST MIRIAM.

MIRIAM?

62

WHERE WAS MIRIAM? EVA SEARCHED.

SHE WENT FROM BARRACKS TO BARRACKS CRAWLING UNDER BUNKS. LOOKING BEHIND DOORS. ASKING, ASKING, ASKING...

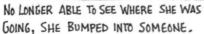

MIRIAM?

TWENTY-FOUR HOURS AND NO MIRIAM. EVA WAS DESPERATE.

NO LONGER ABLE TO SEE WHERE SHE WAS GOING, SHE BUMPED INTO SOMEONE.

MIRIAM! THE TWINS' JOY WAS BEYOND ALL BOUNDS. HUGS, KISSES, A SHARED PIECE OF CHOCOLATE SOMEONE HAD GIVEN TO MIRIAM. NEVER, NEVER AGAIN WOULD THEY BE SEPARATED THEY PLEDGED.

FOR NINE DAYS, THE GIRLS SCRABBLED AND SCAVENGED ON THEIR OWN IN THE WINTER CAMP.

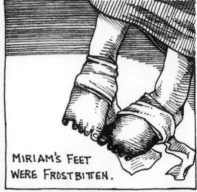

MIRIAM'S FEET WERE FROSTBITTEN.

THEY BROKE INTO THE SS QUARTERS. FOOD WAS SPILLING OUT OF CABINETS. SO MUCH FOOD, BUT IT WOULDN'T BE TOUCHED. RUMOR HAD IT THAT IT HAD BEEN POISONED BY THE RETREATING NAZIS. ONE FINAL CRUELTY.

AT LAST FINDING THE KITCHENS, EVA AND MIRIAM DINED ON SAUERKRAUT IN HUGE BARRELS QUENCHING THEIR THIRST WITH THE JUICE.

AND HOMEMADE MATZO BAKED ON NEWLY FIRED STOVES.

BUT OVEREATING AFTER WEEKS AND MONTHS OF DEPRIVATION BECAME A NEW DANGER. ONE GIRL WHO HAD JOINED THEM DIED FROM TOO MUCH, TOO SOON.

THE VISTULA RIVER WAS THE CLOSEST WATER SUPPLY. IN JANUARY, THE RIVER WAS COVERED WITH ICE.

EVA AND MIRIAM AND ANOTHER SET OF TWINS CARRIED THEIR BUCKETS DOWN TO THE BANK.

ON THE OTHER SIDE WAS A GIRL. A VISION OF NORMALITY IN A CLEAN WINTER COAT, SHINY BLOND HAIR IN CAREFUL BRAIDS, A SCHOOL BAG SLUNG OVER A SHOULDER.

WHAT? HOW? WHY? COULD THERE BE A WORLD OUTSIDE THE CAMP? A WORLD NOT DEFINED BY TERRIBLE LOSS, SUFFERING, FILTH AND LICE? A WORLD THAT EXISTED WITHOUT LITTLE GIRLS BEING TORTURED BY MONSTROUS EXPERIMENTS?

ANGER WAS THE ONLY RATIONAL RESPONSE.

THE LITTLE GIRL WAS NEVER SEEN AGAIN.

THE WAR HAD NOT LEFT, BATTLES RAGED ALL AROUND.

AND THE NAZIS RETURNED TO DESTROY MORE AND MORE EVIDENCE OF THEIR CRIMES. FIRES BURNED, SHOTS RANG OUT. THE UNENDING NOISE AND CONFUSION OF WAR.

DR. MENGELE RETURNED ON JANUARY 18, 1945, AND FLED WITH TWO BOXES OF FILES, THE RECORDS OF THREE THOUSAND TWINS HE HAD EXPERIMENTED ON. RECORDS THAT HAVE NEVER BEEN SEEN AGAIN.

AND ANOTHER NINE DAYS OF SEARCHING, SCROUNGING, CLINGING TO LIFE FOR THE TWINS AND THE OTHER INHABITANTS OF THE CAMP.

THE SNOW FELL THE MORNING OF JANUARY 27, 1945. BUT EVEN THE FRESH COAT OF WHITE COULDN'T HIDE THE DIRTY GRAYNESS OF THE CAMP.

AT 3:00 OR 4:00 PM A WOMAN CRIED OVER AND OVER:

WE ARE FREE! WE ARE FREE!

SOMETHING WAS COMING THROUGH THE SNOWFALL. SOLDIERS! NO, NOT RETURNING NAZIS.

THESE SOLDIERS HAD DIFFERENT UNIFORMS AND WERE CLOAKED IN SNOW CAMOUFLAGED CAPES. THE SOVIET ARMY HAD ARRIVED TO LIBERATE AUSCHWITZ!

HUGS, SMILES, COOKIES, CHOCOLATE!

ШОКОЛАД

AN ACCORDION PLAYED. AND SOLDIERS DANCED. A FEW OF THE NEWLY FREED CAPTIVES ATTEMPTED TO JOIN IN.

EVA AND MIRIAM PEEKED OUT FROM THEIR BUNK. THEY WERE ALMOST AFRAID TO BELIEVE THEIR IMPRISONMENT AND TORTURE WERE OVER.

THEIR TEN MONTHS IN HELL. TEN MONTHS THAT WERE A MIRACLE TO SURVIVE. WHAT NEXT? BACK TO THE FARM? BACK TO FIND MAMA, PAPA, EDIT, AND ALIZ? BACK TO WHAT HAD EXISTED BEFORE THE NIGHTMARE BEGAN?

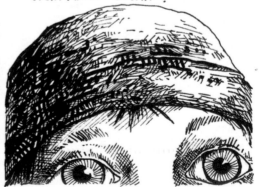

THE SOVIETS DOCUMENTED THE CAMP.

CAMERAS CLICKED TO RECORD THE UNBURNED, UNBURIED BODIES THAT WERE STACKED LIKE RICKS OF WOOD OR LEFT TO LIE WHERE THEIR LAST BREATH WAS TAKEN.

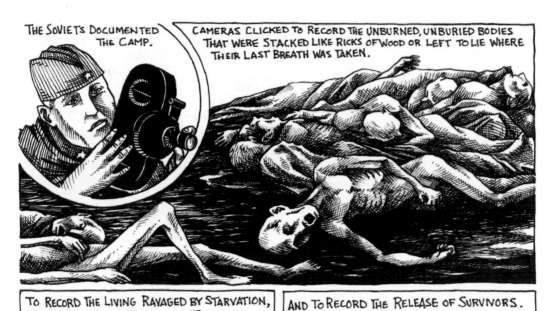

TO RECORD THE LIVING RAVAGED BY STARVATION, DEPRIVATION, DISEASE, AND TORTURE.

AND TO RECORD THE RELEASE OF SURVIVORS.

YEARS LATER, EVA FOUND HERSELF AND MIRIAM IN THESE FILMS, DRESSED IN THE OVERSIZED STRIPED UNIFORMS THEY NEVER WORE BUT WERE GIVEN FOR THE FILMING, MARCHING BETWEEN FENCES THAT LED AROUND AND NOT OUT OF THE CAMP. FILMS OF RELEASE SHOT SEVERAL WEEKS AFTER THE ACTUAL LIBERATION AND MEANT TO SERVE AS SOVIET PROPAGANDA, BUT STILL POIGNANT FOR ALL OF THAT, BECAUSE THEY REPRESENTED THE END OF AUSCHWITZ, OF BIRKENAU, THE END OF THE NIGHTMARE THAT LEFT SO MANY INNOCENTS DEAD, ABUSED, AND TRAUMATIZED.

THE NIGHTMARE ENDURED FOR TEN MONTHS BY THE MOZES TWINS.

THE NIGHTMARE SURVIVED BY EVA AND MIRIAM.

Chapter 4: The Way Home

They stayed in the camp for another two weeks. They worried about food, but the Soviet soldiers fed them bean soup. So much soup they had to be careful not to overeat.

Finally a man took the twins into his horsecart with as many other children as he could fit and drove to the nearby city of Katowice.

Another few weeks in a refugee camp. It was arranged by the Soviet Army and International Red Cross that the girls be taken to an orphanage run by Catholic nuns. A nun took the Mozes twins to their room and a bed covered with clean, white sheets.

Too clean, too white for girls dirty and covered with lice. The twins stripped the sheets from the bed and slept on the bare mattress.

THE NUNS WERE KIND AND GAVE THEM TOYS. THE GIRLS TOSSED THEM AWAY. THEY HAD BEEN THROUGH HELL AND WERE NO LONGER CHILDREN.

THE WALLS OF THE ORPHANAGE WERE COVERED WITH CRUCIFIXES AND ICONS. THE GIRLS TURNED AWAY FOR PAPA WOULD NEVER APPROVE.

ALL THEY WANTED WAS TO BE HOME. THEY MET WITH THE MOTHER SUPERIOR OF THE ORPHANAGE TO MAKE THEIR PLEA.

THERE WOULD BE A WAY. *EVA WOULD NOT GIVE UP.*

MOTHER SUPERIOR, WE MUST FIND OUR FAMILY.

NO, YOU GIRLS ARE ORPHANS.

A GIRL HAD TOLD THEM THAT THE STREETCARS WERE FREE FOR SURVIVORS OF THE CAMP. THEIR TATTOOED NUMBER WAS THE TICKET.

EVERYDAY, THE GIRLS RODE THE STREETCARS SEARCHING, SEARCHING, SEARCHING...

EVENTUALLY, THE MOZES TWINS FOUND THE DISPLACED PERSONS CAMP AND MRS. CSENGERI AND HER TWINS.

MRS. CSENGERI AGREED TO TELL THE NUNS THAT EVA AND MIRIAM WERE HER NIECES.

THE GIRLS MOVED INTO THE CAMP TO SHARE A TENT WITH THE CSENGERIS AND MRS. GOLDENTHAL AND HER TWINS, ALEX AND ERNO (WHO JUST HAPPENED TO BE THE SAME AGE AS EVA AND MIRIAM), AND HER YOUNG DAUGHTER, MARGARITA.

MARGARITA HAD SURVIVED THE CAMP BECAUSE HER MOTHER HAD HER FIRST HIDDEN UNDER HER DRESS AND THEN UNDER THE MATTRESS IN THE BARRACKS.

AFTER A MONTH IN THE CAMP, THE TWINS, WEARING NEW DRESSES SEWN FROM OLD RED ARMY UNIFORMS, LEFT WITH THE FAMILIES.

THEY TRAVELED BACK TO ROMANIA THE WAY THEY HAD COME, IN A CATTLE CAR, BUT THIS CATTLE CAR HAD BEEN CONVERTED TO TRANSPORT SOVIET SOLDIERS AND FITTED WITH BUNK BEDS.

WHEN THE TRAIN PERIODICALLY STOPPED, THE FAMILIES GOT OFF TO COOK AND TAKE FREE BREATHS IN A GLORIOUS SPRINGTIME.

THEY PASSED VILLAGES IN RUINS AND BURNT FIELDS BUT ALWAYS WITH THE HOPE OF RETURNING HOME TO THE FARM AND THEIR REUNITED FAMILY.

THE TRAIN'S DESTINATION WAS A REFUGEE CAMP ON THE OUTSKIRTS OF CZERNOWITZ, UKRAINE, ON THE ROMANIAN BORDER, WHERE THEY WOULD STAY FOR THE NEXT TWO MONTHS.

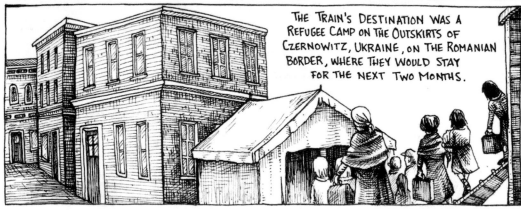

THEN BACK ON THE TRAIN TO ANOTHER REFUGEE CAMP IN SLUTZ. AND ANOTHER COUPLE OF MONTHS. THEN ON TO NAGYVÁRAD WHERE THE GOLDENTHALS DEPARTED.

FINALLY, THEY ARRIVED IN ŞIMLEU SILVANIEI, THE HOME OF THE CSENGERIS AND THE BEGINNING OF THE MOZESES' EXPERIENCE OF DISPLACEMENT, TORTURE, AND LOSS.

THE NEXT DAY, THEY SAID GOODBYE TO MRS. CSENGERI, WHO HAD DONE SO MUCH TO HELP THEM, AND HEADED BACK TO PORTZ AND THEIR HOPES OF RECONCILIATION WITH THE REST OF THE MOZES FAMILY.

ARRIVING, THE TWINS WALKED DOWN THE VILLAGE'S MAIN STREET. NO ONE GREETED THEM. ALL WAS SILENT BUT FOR THE WHISPERS BEHIND WINDOWS AND CLOSED DOORS.

HOME!

THE FLOWER GARDEN WAS OVERGROWN WITH WEEDS.

THE HOUSE WAS EMPTY, STRIPPED BARE. NO MAMA AND PAPA, NO EDIT AND ALIZ.

THE ONLY FRIENDLY VOICE THE GIRLS HEARD WAS MAMA'S DACHSHUND, LILY, RUSHING TO WELCOME THEM BACK.

THE ONLY THINGS THE GIRLS COULD FIND FROM THEIR FORMER FAMILY LIFE WERE THREE PHOTOS.

EDIT, ALIZ, AND THREE COUSINS.   A PHOTO FROM 1942 OF EVA WITH HER TEACHERS. THE WHOLE MOZES FAMILY WITH EVA AND MIRIAM IN THE BURGUNDY DRESSES THEY WORE INTO AUSCHWITZ.

THE HOME WAS DESOLATE. EVEN THE APPLE TREES HAD BEEN RANSACKED.

THE RED CROSS TRACED THE TWINS' COUSIN SHMILU TO COME AND GET THEM.

SHMILU WAS THE TWENTY-YEAR-OLD SON OF PAPA'S SISTER IRENA. HE AND IRENA HAD SURVIVED WHILE THE REST OF THE FAMILY HAD NOT.

PAPA, MAMA, EDIT, AND ALIZ HAD NOT SURVIVED.

THEY STAYED FOR A SHORT WHILE IN THE FARM'S SUMMER KITCHEN WITH BORROWED FURNITURE AND DONATED FOOD.

COUSIN SHMILU, WHO WOULD RETURN TO THE FARM AND TRY TO RESTORE IT, TRAVELED WITH THE GIRLS TO THE CITY OF CLUJ, ROMANIA. THERE THEY WOULD LIVE WITH HIS MOTHER, THEIR NEW GUARDIAN.

AUNT IRENA HAD A CERTAIN SOCIAL STANDING BEFORE THE WAR, HAVING BEEN WELL-TO-DO ENOUGH TO HAVE TRAVELED TO THE RIVIERA AND MONTE CARLO. EVEN UNDER THE SOVIETS, SHE WAS ALLOWED TO RETAIN SOME OF HER WEALTH BEING BOTH A CAMP SURVIVOR AND A WAR WIDOW.

SOME OF HER PERSIAN RUGS, FINE PORCELAIN, AND SOME DESIGNER FASHIONS REMAINED IN HER KEEPING.

MOST IMPORTANT, SHE WAS ALLOWED TO KEEP HER LARGE APARTMENT BUILDING.

UNFORTUNATELY, HER POSSESSIONS SEEMED TO BE MORE VALUED THAN THE MOZES TWINS FOR WHOM SHE WAS NOW RESPONSIBLE. THEY WERE FED, CLOTHED, AND SHELTERED, BUT THE AFFECTION AND LOVE THESE TORTURED GIRLS SO BADLY NEEDED WERE NOT PRESENT IN THE WELL-APPOINTED APARTMENT.

79

THE GIRLS STRUGGLED WITH WHAT IS NOW RECOGNIZED AS POST-TRAUMATIC STRESS DISORDER (PTSD). HORRIBLE NIGHTMARES FILLED WITH GIANT RATS, CORPSES, AND GLEAMING NEEDLES. A BAR OF SOAP COULD BECOME AN OBJECT OF TERROR. THE NAZIS WERE RUMORED TO HAVE USED THE FAT FROM MURDERED JEWS IN

THE MANUFACTURE OF SOAPS. EVA WOULD SOMETIMES SUFFER AUDITORY HALLUCINATIONS WHEN SHE IMAGINED HEARING MAMA AND PAPA'S VOICES CRYING FROM THE BAR.

AND THEN HEALTH PROBLEMS: ENDLESS COLDS, SORES THAT GREW TO BURSTING AND LEFT SCARS.

EVEN A KINDLY DOCTOR WITH HIS PRESCRIPTION OF GOOD FOOD AND VITAMINS TO DEAL WITH THEIR MALNUTRITION WAS A FIGURE OF TERROR.

AUNT IRENA REMARRIED ANOTHER SURVIVOR, A PHARMACIST.

BUT HER NEW HUSBAND DISAPPEARED ONE DAY, AS WAS NOT UNCOMMON IN THE NEW WORLD OF THE SOVIET SATELLITE NATIONS.

RATIONS WERE TIGHT BUT AUGMENTED BY SHMILU BRINGING PRODUCE (VEGETABLES AND EGGS) FROM THE FARM.

EVA WAS SPOTTED EATING WHITE BREAD ON THE BALCONY ONE DAY, AND SOON AFTER, THE POLICE RAIDED THE APARTMENT, CONFISCATING ALL UNAUTHORIZED FOOD.

A SECRET CABINET HAD TO BE BUILT SO FOOD COULD BE STORED AWAY FROM PRYING EYES.

LIFE WAS NO EASIER OUTSIDE THE APARTMENT. THE GIRLS WERE TAUNTED WITH STORIES OF JEWISH VAMPIRES SUCKING THE BLOOD OF CHRISTIAN GIRLS.

engedelmeskedik

HUNGARIAN WAS THE ONLY LANGUAGE AT SCHOOL, LEAVING THE ROMANIAN-SPEAKING GIRLS BEHIND.

THE GIRLS STARTED EATING DINNER AT A NEARBY ORPHANAGE BECAUSE OF THE LACK OF SUSTENANCE AT HOME.

ON THE WAY HOME, THEY WORRIED THAT THE JEWISH VAMPIRE MIGHT THINK THEY WERE CHRISTIAN AND DRAW THEIR BLOOD TOO.

CLOTHING AND THE OTHER NECESSITIES OF LIFE HAD TO BE FOUGHT FOR. LUCKILY, AUNT IRENA HAD CONTACTS IN SEVERAL PLACES WHO OCCASIONALLY KEPT COMPLETE DEPRIVATION FROM BECOMING THE NORM.

PALESTINE BECAME THE STATE OF ISRAEL IN 1948, AND UNCLE AARON'S LETTERS MADE RELOCATION FOR THE TWINS MORE AND MORE APPEALING. UNCLE AARON, PAPA'S BROTHER, HAD IMMIGRATED THERE BEFORE THE WAR AND ESTABLISHED A HOME FAR AWAY FROM THE NAZIS.

DREAMS OF THIS NEW LAND DANCED IN EVA'S HEAD.

BOUNTIFUL FOOD!

ORANGES GROWING LIKE APPLES IN THEIR OLD ORCHARDS.

CHOCOLATE! EVEN CHOCOLATE!

AUNT IRENA RECEIVED A LETTER, A MISSING SON WAS ALIVE THERE!

SHE IMMEDIATELY GOT HER VISA, BUT IT WOULD TAKE EVA AND MIRIAM TWO LONG YEARS TO RECEIVE THEIRS. THE SOVIETS WANTED ALL THE YOUTH TO REBUILD THE WAR-RAVAGED LANDS OF EASTERN EUROPE.

ANTICIPATION FOR THE EVENTUAL MOVE GREW. A YEAR BEFORE LEAVING, EVERYONE WAS PACKED AND READY TO DEPART.

SO READY THAT EVA, HAVING BEEN CALLED INTO A COMMUNIST PARTY OFFICE FOR SOME MINOR INFRACTION, RESOUNDINGLY STATED:

THIS IS YOUR PARTY, NOT MY PARTY!

THE FARM IN PORTZ WAS TURNED OVER TO THE GOVERNMENT.

AUNT IRENA'S HUSBAND HAD BEEN RELEASED FROM JAIL (REMAINING FOREVER SILENT ABOUT HIS CAPTIVITY).

Casă dulce Casă

JUNE 1950: THE FAMILY WAS READY TO GO, TAKING ONLY WHAT THEY COULD WEAR.

84

THEY TOOK THE TRAIN TO CONSTANŢA ON THE COAST OF THE BLACK SEA.

THREE THOUSAND PEOPLE CROWDED ONTO A SHIP WITH ONLY ENOUGH ROOM FOR A THOUSAND AND WAITED FOR A LONG DAY TO SET SAIL.

THE VOYAGE WAS PUNCTUATED WITH THE SALT BREEZES OF THE MEDITERRANEAN AND THE JOYOUS COMPANY OF DOLPHINS.

FINALLY, THE SHIP DOCKED IN HAIFA WITH THE SUNRISE GLEAMING ON THE SLOPES OF MOUNT CARMEL.

THE PASSENGERS BROKE SPONTANEOUSLY INTO SONG, THE "HATIKVAH" THE NATIONAL ANTHEM OF THEIR NEW HOME ISRAEL!

AS LONG AS WITHIN OUR HEARTS THE JEWISH SOUL SINGS, AS LONG AS FORWARD TO THE EAST, *TO ZION...*

UNCLE AARON GREETED THEM WITH TEARS AND HUGS.

THE TWINS WERE SIXTEEN YEARS OLD, AND THEY WERE SAFE.

EVA AND MIRIAM WERE GIVEN A PLACE IN THE YOUTH ALIYAH VILLAGE, A KIBBUTZ OF THREE HUNDRED TEENAGERS.

עלית הנוער

THEY ATTENDED SCHOOL HALF A DAY AND

FARMED THE OTHER HALF - RAISING TOMATOES AND PEANUTS AND MILKING COWS.

THE TWINS ALSO EMBRACED THEIR JEWISHNESS IN THIS NEW YET ANCIENT HOMELAND: LEARNING HEBREW, HONORING SHABBAT, AND DANCING THE HORA.

שלום

SNUGGLED IN THEIR LITTLE DORM ROOM, THEY SLEPT PEACEFULLY FOR THE FIRST TIME IN YEARS.

IN 1952, THE MOZES TWINS WERE CONSCRIPTED INTO THE ISRAELI ARMY AS PART OF THE COUNTRY'S COMPULSORY SERVICE.

MIRIAM BECAME A REGISTERED NURSE.

EVA LEARNED DRAFTING AND REMAINED IN THE ARMY FOR THE NEXT EIGHT YEARS, EVENTUALLY EARNING THE RANK OF SERGEANT MAJOR.

IN APRIL OF 1960, EVA MET ANOTHER YOUNG SURVIVOR, AN AMERICAN VISITING HIS BROTHER: MICHAEL "MICKEY" KOR.

MICKEY HAD GROWN UP IN RIGA, LATVIA, WITH HIS PARENTS AND BROTHERS. IN AUGUST OF 1941, AFTER THE NAZI INVASION OF LATVIA, ALL THE JEWS WERE FORCED INTO THE GHETTO.

MICKEY'S MOTHER PACKED A WHITE TABLECLOTH EMBROIDERED WITH RED FLOWERS AND CONTINUED TO USE IT FOR EVERY MEAL NO MATTER HOW MEAGER. WHEN QUESTIONED ABOUT THE ABSURDITY OF PRISONERS DINING WITH SUCH AN AMENITY, SHE DECLARED, "WE ARE HUMANS! WE ARE CIVILIZED!"

THE FAMILY WAS CONTINUOUSLY SAVAGED BY THE NAZIS. ONE BROTHER, A SAILOR, WAS THROWN OVERBOARD TO DROWN. MICKEY'S FATHER WAS BEATEN TO DEATH IN THE STREET.

IN NOVEMBER OF 1941, THE INHABITANTS OF THE GHETTO WERE SEPARATED INTO ABLE-BODIED MEN (MICKEY'S MOTHER PUSHED HIM INTO THIS GROUP) AND ALL OTHERS. THE MEN WERE MARCHED OFF TO WORK CAMPS, AND THE NAZI EXECUTION SQUADS MACHINE-GUNNED ALL THE OTHERS.

MICKEY WAS FIRST SENT TO BUCHENWALD, MOVED TO STUTTHOF (A CAMP NEAR GDANSK, POLAND), AND THEN TO THE WORK CAMP AT MAGDEBURG, GERMANY.

THE NAZIS WERE LOSING THE WAR IN 1944, AND TO COVER UP THEIR CRIMES, THE DEATH MARCHES OF PRISONERS BEGAN. MICKEY, SENSING HIS CHANCE, ESCAPED AND HID.

HE WAS LIBERATED BY THE US'S 250 ENGINEER COMBAT BATTALION AND TAKEN UNDER THE WING OF LT. COL. ANDREW NEHF. NEHF SUPPORTED MICKEY'S IMMIGRATION TO THE UNITED STATES IN 1946. MICKEY ENDED HIS LONG JOURNEY IN TERRE HAUTE, INDIANA.

HE FINISHED HIS SCHOOLING AT PURDUE UNIVERSITY IN PHARMACY AND IN 1960 TRAVELED TO VISIT A SURVIVING BROTHER IN ISRAEL, WHERE HE MET EVA.

EVA AND HE HAD NO COMMON LANGUAGE   OTHER THAN THE LANGUAGE OF THE HEART.

CHAPTER 5: FORGIVENESS

TERRE HAUTE, IN THE HEART OF THE INDUSTRIAL MIDWEST HAD IN YEARS PAST BEEN A RAILROAD HUB WITH A THRIVING UNION WORKFORCE, BUT NOW WITH THE ADVENT OF HIGHWAYS AND 18-WHEELERS, IT HAD BEGUN TO SEE A DECLINE. IT STILL RETAINED INDIANA STATE UNIVERSITY AND REMAINED A CENTER OF THE REGIONAL ECONOMY.

MICKEY HAD THOUGHT THAT EVA WAS A QUIET GIRL, BUT AFTER THREE MONTHS STUDYING ENGLISH BY WAY OF TELEVISION AND THEN SECURING A JOB WITH HER NEWFOUND SKILL, HE LEARNED HIS NEW WIFE WAS ANYTHING BUT DEMURE.

EVENTUALLY, EVA BECAME A SUCCESSFUL REAL ESTATE AGENT DUE IN NO SMALL PART TO HER VERBAL SKILLS AND PERSUASIVE POWERS.

MARRIAGE ALSO BROUGHT A GROWING FAMILY. ALEX ON APRIL 15, 1961.

AND RINA ON MARCH 1, 1963.

BUT WITH ALL THE HAPPINESS AND SECURITY (AND AN AMERICAN CITIZENSHIP IN 1965) IN THIS NEW LIFE, EVA WAS HAUNTED.

THERE WERE NIGHTMARES. CELEBRATIONS WERE ALWAYS WITHOUT GRANDPARENTS AND EXTENDED FAMILY.

HALLOWEEN WAS ESPECIALLY HARD WITH PRANKSTERS, SOMETIMES INNOCENT

AND SOMETIMES MALICIOUSLY IGNORANT.

ALEX WAS ASHAMED.

WHY CAN'T YOU BE A *NORMAL* MOTHER?

EVA KNEW SHE HAD TO SHARE HER STORY, BUT HOW?

YEARS WENT BY WITHOUT AN ANSWER, AND THEN SUDDENLY, THE ANSWER PRESENTED ITSELF. IN APRIL OF 1978, NBC TELEVISION ANNOUNCED IT WOULD BROADCAST A SPECIAL FOUR-PART SERIES: *THE HOLOCAUST.*

THE HOLOCAUST WAS THE FIRST MAJOR TELEVISION PRODUCTION TO TACKLE THE HISTORY OF THE TRAGIC RISE AND CONSEQUENCES OF NAZISM IN GERMANY, FOCUSING PRIMARILY ON THE EXPERIENCE OF A FICTIONAL JEWISH FAMILY.

EVA, AS A KNOWN SURVIVOR, WAS ASKED BY TERRE HAUTE'S NBC AFFILIATE WTWO TO APPEAR ON THE NEWS AFTER THE BROADCAST TO TELL HER STORY.

HER FIRST APPEARANCE WAS MET WITH SUCH INTEREST THAT SHE WAS ASKED BACK THE NEXT EVENING TO MAKE FURTHER COMMENTS.

THE WORD WAS OUT.
NOT ONLY WAS EVA'S STORY
IMPORTANT AND
NECESSARY, BUT EVA WAS
A WONDERFUL AND
COMPELLING SPEAKER.
AND FOR THE FIRST TIME,
EVA HAD A SENSE OF
HONORING AND NURTURING
THAT LITTLE GIRL EVA
WHO HAD SUFFERED
SUCH TERRIBLE
LOSS AND TORTURE.
EVA AND EVA
HAD BECOME ONE.

SHE STARTED
RECEIVING REQUESTS
TO SPEAK. SCHOOLS,
COMMUNITY
GROUPS,
RELIGIOUS
ORGANIZATIONS
...

PEOPLE NEEDED TO HEAR EVA.
BUT ...

SOMETHING WAS MISSING. EVA WAS NOT AN EXPERT ON AUSCHWITZ, BIRKENAU, OR THE TERRIBLE MACHINERY OF THE DEATH CAMPS. SHE WAS, HOWEVER, AN EXPERT ON HER EXPERIENCE, A SURVIVOR OF MENGELE'S TWIN EXPERIMENTS. WITH ALL THE REVIVED INTEREST, IT SEEMED THE SUFFERING OF THE TWINS WAS SO OFTEN FORGOTTEN. EVA WROTE TO NEWSPAPERS, MAGAZINES, GOVERNMENT AGENCIES TRYING TO GET SOME ATTENTION FOR THE MENGELE TWINS, BUT ALWAYS SEEMED TO COME UP AGAINST A BLANK WALL.

EVA KNEW THAT THERE WERE ONE HUNDRED AND EIGHTY TO TWO HUNDRED SURVIVING TWINS, SO SHE WROTE THEM AS WELL, BUT STILL NO RESPONSE.

CANDLES

THEY WOULDN'T LISTEN TO HER AS AN INDIVIDUAL, BUT MAYBE THEY WOULD LISTEN TO AN ORGANIZATION. ON FEBRUARY 21, 1984, SHE AND HER SISTER MIRIAM FOUNDED AN ORGANIZATION ORIGINALLY CALLED ALL TWINS - AUSCHWITZ LAB'S LIVING TWINS WORLD INSTITUTE & NETWORK OF SURVIVORS. THEY SOON CHANGED THE NAME TO CANDLES - CHILDREN OF AUSCHWITZ NAZI DEADLY LAB EXPERIMENTS SURVIVORS. EVA WAS RIGHT: THEY STARTED TO LISTEN.

LUCETTE LAGNADO, AN ASSISTANT FOR THE WELL-KNOWN COLUMNIST JACK ANDERSON, RESPONDED TO THE LETTER. SHE GOT THE STORY TO ANDERSON, AND HE WROTE A COVER STORY FOR *PARADE MAGAZINE* ON SEPTEMBER 2, 1984.

THE MAGAZINE ARRIVED IN THE SUNDAY PAPERS ON MILLIONS OF AMERICAN DOORSTEPS. ACROSS THE COUNTRY, PEOPLE WERE LEARNING THE STORY. NOW, HOPEFULLY, THERE WOULD BE A RESPONSE.

Sunday Paper SEPT. 2, 1984

PARADE

The Twins Of Auschwitz Today

BY JACK ANDERSON

EVA MOZES

IN ISRAEL, SHLOMO KOR PLACED ADS IN THE ISRAELI NEWSPAPERS LOOKING FOR SURVIVORS. EIGHTY TWINS GOT IN CONTACT. ALL OF THEM WERE INVITED TO COME WITH CANDLES TO AUSCHWITZ TO BE THERE TOGETHER FOR THE FORTIETH ANNIVERSARY OF THE LIBERATION.

THIRTY-EIGHT THOUSAND DOLLARS WAS RAISED TO PAY FOR EXPENSES. FOUR JOINED EVA AND MIRIAM. SIX CANDLES WERE LIT IN REMEMBRANCE.

ARBEIT MACHT FREI

ALTHOUGH EVA WAS BEING ASKED TO SPEAK ABOUT HER EXPERIENCE AND THE EXPERIMENTATIONS ON THE TWINS, THERE WAS STILL A LACK OF WIDER RECOGNITION FOR WHAT THE CHILDREN SUFFERED. HER FRUSTRATION AND ANGER GREW, THE ANGER THAT EMBARRASSED HER CHILDREN AT EASTER CELEBRATIONS, AT LITTLE LEAGUE GAMES, THAT SOMETIMES SEPARATED HER FROM HER OWN PLAYFUL NATURE.

THEN IN 1985, WORD CAME THAT AUTHORITIES IN BRAZIL HAD EXHUMED A BODY BURIED UNDER THE NAME OF WOLFGANG GERHARD, AND GERHARD WAS ACTUALLY JOSEF MENGELE.

MENGELE SUFFERED A STROKE WHILE SWIMMING OFF THE COAST IN 1979.

HE HAD ESCAPED EUROPE IN 1945 AND HAD BEEN LIVING FIRST IN ARGENTINA, THEN PARAGUAY, AND FINALLY BRAZIL UNTIL HIS DEATH.

HE DIED WITHOUT ADMITTING, EXPLAINING WHAT HE HAD DONE TO THE CHILDREN. THE SURGERIES, THE INJECTIONS, THE BARBARIC PROCEDURES WOULD REMAIN A MYSTERY.

AUSCHWITZ/BIRKENAU
ZWILLINGSEXPERIMENTE

THE VOLCANO RUMBLING IN EVA'S SOUL WAS NEARING ERUPTION. MAY 7, 1986, THE DAYS OF REMEMBRANCE HOLOCAUST MEMORIAL IN THE US CAPITOL ROTUNDA, ELIE WIESEL WAS SPEAKING, AND EVA EXPLODED!

EVA WAS NOT ARRESTED, BUT SHE SUFFERED A ROTATOR CUFF INJURY TO HER SHOULDER, SEVERE PSYCHOLOGICAL TRAUMA, AND PARIAH STATUS AMONG THE SURVIVOR COMMUNITY.

HATE MAIL CAME IN, AND INVITATIONS DRIED UP. FAMILY LIFE WAS STRAINED. AND THEN EVA RECEIVED AN URGENT CALL FROM ISRAEL.

IN 1987, MIRIAM'S KIDNEYS FAILED. WHATEVER HAD BEEN INJECTED INTO HER WHILE EVA WAS IN THE INFIRMARY THOSE MANY YEARS AGO HAD STUNTED THE GROWTH IN HER KIDNEYS; THEY HADN'T GROWN PAST THE SIZE OF A TEN-YEAR-OLD'S. SHE HAD TO HAVE A TRANSPLANT IMMEDIATELY.

EVA FLEW TO ISRAEL TO ONCE AGAIN RESCUE MIRIAM. THE OPERATION WAS SUCCESSFUL, BUT EVA HAD TO GO HOME TO HER BRUISED SITUATIONS AND HER EMOTIONAL DISTRESS.

BUT LIFE CONTINUED. EVA WENT TO WORK IN REAL ESTATE AGAIN. RELATIONSHIPS, ALTHOUGH OFTEN DIFFICULT, RETURNED. A FEW SPEAKING ENGAGEMENTS FOUND THEIR WAY TO HER.

IN 1993, EVA WAS INVITED TO BOSTON TO SPEAK AT A CONFERENCE DISCUSSING MEDICAL ETHICS. SHE WAS ASKED IF SHE COULD HAVE A NAZI DOCTOR JOIN HER IN THE DISCUSSION.

IN LATER YEARS, SHE JOKED,

WHAT? I HAVEN'T SEEN THAT LISTING IN THE YELLOW PAGES.

SHE REMEMBERED SEEING A DOCUMENTARY IN WHICH A DR. HANS MUNCH, A DOCTOR WHO HAD BEEN AT AUSCHWITZ, WAS FEATURED. EVA TRACKED HIM DOWN, AND HE CONSENTED TO VIDEOTAPE AN INTERVIEW WITH HER.

BEFORE EVA COULD MEET WITH DR. MUNCH IN JULY, THE MONTH OF JUNE HELD THE GREATEST SADNESS OF HER LIFE. ON JUNE 6, HER DEAR SISTER, WHOM SHE HAD PROTECTED AND WHO HAD SHARED HER STRUGGLES AND SURVIVAL, DIED IN ASHKELON, ISRAEL.

FOLLOWING JEWISH CUSTOM, MIRIAM WAS BURIED THE NEXT DAY, WHICH DID NOT ALLOW EVA ENOUGH TIME TO BE THERE TO SAY A FINAL GOODBYE TO THE SISTER SHE HAD ENTERED THE WORLD WITH. EVA MOURNED AND CONTINUED WITH NEW PURPOSE.

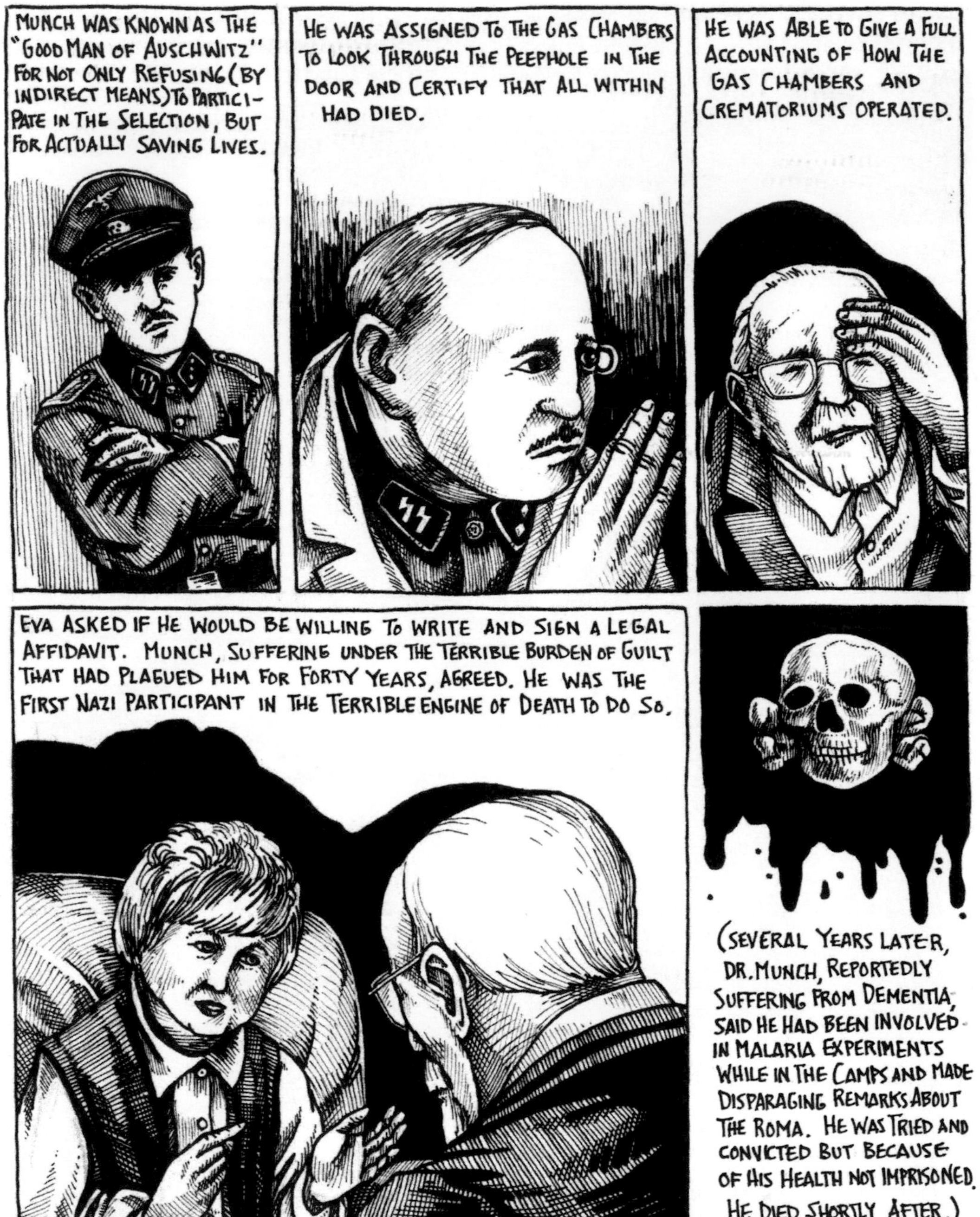
MUNCH WAS KNOWN AS THE "GOOD MAN OF AUSCHWITZ" FOR NOT ONLY REFUSING (BY INDIRECT MEANS) TO PARTICI-PATE IN THE SELECTION, BUT FOR ACTUALLY SAVING LIVES.
HE WAS ASSIGNED TO THE GAS CHAMBERS TO LOOK THROUGH THE PEEPHOLE IN THE DOOR AND CERTIFY THAT ALL WITHIN HAD DIED.
HE WAS ABLE TO GIVE A FULL ACCOUNTING OF HOW THE GAS CHAMBERS AND CREMATORIUMS OPERATED.
EVA ASKED IF HE WOULD BE WILLING TO WRITE AND SIGN A LEGAL AFFIDAVIT. MUNCH, SUFFERING UNDER THE TERRIBLE BURDEN OF GUILT THAT HAD PLAGUED HIM FOR FORTY YEARS, AGREED. HE WAS THE FIRST NAZI PARTICIPANT IN THE TERRIBLE ENGINE OF DEATH TO DO SO.
(SEVERAL YEARS LATER, DR. MUNCH, REPORTEDLY SUFFERING FROM DEMENTIA, SAID HE HAD BEEN INVOLVED IN MALARIA EXPERIMENTS WHILE IN THE CAMPS AND MADE DISPARAGING REMARKS ABOUT THE ROMA. HE WAS TRIED AND CONVICTED BUT BECAUSE OF HIS HEALTH NOT IMPRISONED. HE DIED SHORTLY AFTER.)

EVA RETURNED HOME WITH A COMPLICATED MIX OF FEELINGS; SADNESS, AFFIRMATION, COMPASSION, AND ABOVE ALL, GRATITUDE. GRATITUDE TOWARD A MAN WHO HAD BEEN A PARTICIPANT IN THE HORRENDOUS CRIME OF THE HOLOCAUST BUT WAS FILLED WITH SORROW AND WILLING TO GO ON THE RECORD.

DR. MUNCH HAD GIVEN HER A PROFOUND GIFT, BUT HOW COULD SHE GIVE HER THANKS?

WHILE WASHING DISHES AT HOME ONE EVENING, EVA HAD A SIMPLE BUT INCREDIBLE EPIPHANY: SHE COULD GIVE DR. MUNCH FORGIVENESS!

SHE WANTED TO PUBLICLY FORGIVE DR. MUNCH AS WELL AS PRIVATELY AND PERSONALLY. EVA ENLISTED HER ENGLISH INSTRUCTOR, PROFESSOR SUSAN KAUFMAN, TO SIT WITH HER AND CORRECT THE LETTER OF CLEMENCY.

AS THE LETTER UNFOLDED, DR. KAUFMAN HAD A THOUGHT AND ASKED EVA WHAT TURNED OUT TO BE A LIFE-CHANGING QUESTION:

DR. MUNCH DID NOTHING PHYSICALLY OR DIRECTLY TO YOU: WHY ARE YOU FORGIVING HIM AND NOT DR. MENGELE?

SHOCK! DISMAY! RECOGNITION! IT WAS THE PATH TO FREEDOM, OF LAYING DOWN THE BURDEN OF ANGER, GUILT, OF VICTIMHOOD. FORGIVENESS TO ALL WHO HAD CAUSED HER HARM. FORGIVENESS THAT SAVES ONE'S VERY OWN SOUL. EVA WOULD DO IT.

ON JANUARY 27, 1995, THE FIFTIETH ANNIVERSARY OF THE LIBERATION OF AUSCHWITZ, EVA WITH SON ALEX AND DAUGHTER RINA MET DR. MUNCH WITH HIS DAUGHTER AND GRANDCHILDREN AT THE CAMP.

MUNCH FORMALLY AND IN FRONT OF WITNESSES AND THE WORLD SIGNED HIS AFFIDAVIT ATTESTING TO THE ATROCITIES COMMITTED AND THE EXTERMINATIONS OF JEWS, ROMA, AND ALL THE OTHERS AT AUSCHWITZ AND BIRKENAU BY THE NAZIS.

EVA FOLLOWED WITH HER TESTAMENT OF FORGIVENESS, OF AMNESTY TO THE PERPETRATORS OF THE CRIMES AGAINST HER...

I, EVA MOZES KOR, A TWIN WHO AS A CHILD SURVIVED JOSEF MENGELE'S EXPERIMENTS AT AUSCHWITZ FIFTY YEARS AGO, HEREBY GIVE AMNESTY TO ALL NAZIS WHO PARTICIPATED DIRECTLY OR INDIRECTLY IN THE MURDER OF MY FAMILY AND MILLIONS OF OTHERS.

I, EVA MOZES KOR, IN MY NAME ONLY, GIVE THIS AMNESTY BECAUSE IT IS TIME TO GO ON: IT IS TIME TO HEAL OUR SOULS: IT IS TIME TO FORGIVE, BUT NEVER FORGET.

I AM HEALED INSIDE: THEREFORE, IT GIVES ME NO JOY TO SEE ANY NAZI CRIMINAL IN JAIL, NOR DO I WANT TO SEE ANY HARM COME TO JOSEF MENGELE, OR THE MENGELE FAMILY, OR THEIR BUSINESS CORPORATIONS. I URGE ALL FORMER NAZIS TO COME FORWARD AND TESTIFY TO THE CRIMES THEY HAVE COMMITTED WITHOUT ANY FEAR OF FURTHER PROSECUTION.

HERE IN AUSCHWITZ, I HOPE IN SOME SMALL WAY TO SEND THE WORLD A MESSAGE OF FORGIVENESS, A MESSAGE OF PEACE, A MESSAGE OF HOPE, A MESSAGE OF HEALING.

NO MORE WARS,
NO MORE EXPERIMENTS WITHOUT CONSENT,
NO MORE GAS CHAMBERS,
NO MORE BOMBS,
NO MORE HATRED,
NO MORE KILLING.
NO MORE
AUSCHWITZS.

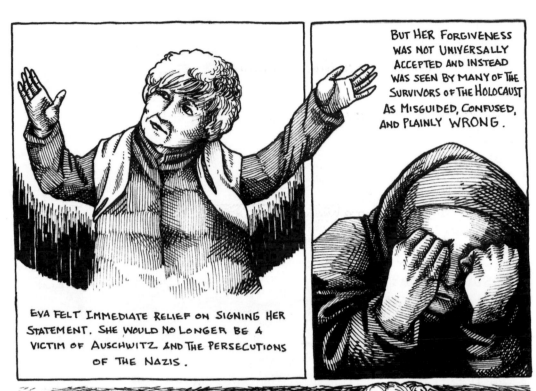

EVA FELT IMMEDIATE RELIEF ON SIGNING HER STATEMENT. SHE WOULD NO LONGER BE A VICTIM OF AUSCHWITZ AND THE PERSECUTIONS OF THE NAZIS.

BUT HER FORGIVENESS WAS NOT UNIVERSALLY ACCEPTED AND INSTEAD WAS SEEN BY MANY OF THE SURVIVORS OF THE HOLOCAUST AS MISGUIDED, CONFUSED, AND PLAINLY WRONG.

EVA WOULD EXPLAIN IN LECTURES AND CONVERSATIONS FOR THE REST OF HER LIFE THAT HER AMNESTY WAS WHAT SHE DID AS A MATTER OF HER PERSONAL SALVATION AND NOT A GENERAL PRINCIPLE THAT EVERYONE COULD OR WOULD EMBRACE. SHE DID, HOWEVER, URGE THAT VICTIMS TRY TO COME TO FORGIVENESS FOR HOW IT WOULD FREE THEM FROM THE CRIMES PERPETRATED ON THEM. IT WAS FOR EVA AND THOSE OTHERS WHO COULD DO IT THE MOST PROFOUND SOURCE OF HEALING.

ON APRIL 30, 1995,
EVA OPENED THE CANDLES
MUSEUM AND EDUCATION CENTER
IN TERRE HAUTE.

LIKE EVA, THE MUSEUM
WAS LITTLE
BUT MIGHTY.

LOCATED IN A
SMALL STRIP MALL,
IT WAS NOT ONLY
THE STATE OF INDIANA'S
SOLE HOLOCAUST MUSEUM
BUT ALSO THE ONLY
MUSEUM IN THE WORLD
DEVOTED TO THE CHILDREN
OF THE NAZI
MEDICAL EXPERIMENTS.

WHEN EVA WAS NOT TALKING
TO VISITORS OF THE MUSEUM,
SHE WAS ON THE ROAD
TALKING TO RELIGIOUS,
FRATERNAL, AND STUDENT
GROUPS, AND ANY
GATHERING THAT
INVITED HER.

WHERE ONCE SHE WAS FILLED
WITH RIGHTEOUS ANGER, SHE
NOW WAS BURSTING WITH A
MESSAGE OF JOY AND
RENEWAL.

BUT EVA DIDN'T JUST TALK: SHE TOOK ACTION.

HER AMNESTY DID NOT EXONERATE ALL COMPANIES WITHOUT RESTITUTION, AND IN 1999, SHE LED A LAWSUIT AGAINST THE CHEMICAL AND PHARMACEUTICAL GIANT BAYER AG (WHICH DURING THE NAZI ERA HAD BEEN OWNED BY THE MASSIVE CONGLOMERATE IG FARBEN THAT HAD ALREADY BEEN FOUND GUILTY OF WAR CRIMES) FOR ITS INVOLVEMENT WITH MENGELE AND HIS EXPERIMENTS AS WELL AS THE SLAVE LABOR USED IN THEIR FACILITIES.

EVA'S SUIT WON, AND THE REMEMBRANCE, RESPONSIBILITY, AND FUTURE FUND WAS AWARDED FIVE BILLION DOLLARS.

EVA NOW BECAME A MUCH SOUGHT AFTER LECTURER ON MEDICAL ETHICS. EVEN SPEAKING AT THE MAX PLANCK SOCIETY ON "BIOMEDICAL SCIENCES AND HUMAN EXPERIMENTATION AT THE KAISER WILHELM INSTITUTE AND THE AUSCHWITZ CONNECTION" IN 2001.

BUT AS HER MESSAGE OF FORGIVENESS AND COMPASSION WAS REACHING SO MANY, TRAGEDY STRUCK. ON NOVEMBER 18, 2003, THE CANDLES MUSEUM WAS FIREBOMBED.

SO MUCH WAS DESTROYED, BUT EVEN GRIEF FROM THIS ANONYMOUS (AND ALWAYS TO REMAIN UNSOLVED) CRIME, EVA PERSEVERED AND A NEW LARGER MUSEUM WAS CONSTRUCTED ON THE GROUNDS OF THE OLD ONE, OPENING ON APRIL 3, 2005.

EVA WAS IN THE MUSEUM AS OFTEN AS SHE COULD BE (WHILE KEEPING A TRAVELING SCHEDULE THAT ENCOMPASSED AUDIENCES LARGE AND SMALL, YOUNG AND OLD, RURAL AND URBAN) LECTURING TWICE A WEEK, ANSWERING QUESTIONS, AND CONVERSING WITH AS MANY PEOPLE AS SHE COULD.

AND IN MARCH OF 2019, EVA WAS ABLE TO CONTINUE THE SAME LECTURING, QUESTIONING, AND CONVERSING EVEN WHEN SHE WASN'T ACTUALLY IN THE MUSEUM BY WAY OF A HOLOGRAM PROVIDED BY STEPHEN SPIELBERG'S SHOAH FOUNDATION (SHOAH IS HEBREW FOR "CATASTROPHE" AND IS A TERM THAT HAS BEEN USED FOR THE HOLOCAUST SINCE THE 1940s). THE FOUNDATION WAS STARTED IN 1994 AFTER SPIELBERG COMPLETED HIS SEMINAL HOLOCAUST FILM *SCHINDLER'S LIST.* ITS PRIMARY PURPOSE WAS TO PRESERVE THE TESTIMONY OF THE SURVIVORS (55,000) OF THE NAZIS BUT HAS EXPANDED TO RECORD THE STORIES OF OTHER GENOCIDES AROUND THE WORLD.

THE HOLOGRAM, OR MORE PROPERLY "INTERACTIVE BIOGRAPHY", IS ONE OF TWENTY-FOUR THE FOUNDATION HAS PRODUCED AND CREATES THE ILLUSION OF HAVING DIRECT AND PERSONAL CONTACT WITH EVA.

No matter where Eva appeared in person, film, or in print, she always presented her hard-won life lessons:

1. Never, ever give up.

2. Prevent Prejudice by judging people only on their actions and the content of their character.

3. Forgive your worst enemy. It will heal your soul and set you free.

4. Give your parents an extra hug and kiss for the children who had or have no parents.

5. Each of us has a part to play in repairing our world. May I be the change I wish to see.

EVA WAS FORTHRIGHT
IN HER DECLARATION:
"ANGER AND HATE ARE
THE SEEDS OF WAR.
FORGIVENESS IS
THE SEED OF PEACE."

EVA DIDN'T JUST DECLARE, SHE PUT WORDS INTO ACTION OVER AND OVER AGAIN... IN THE SPRING OF 2015, SHE MET OSKAR GROENING OUTSIDE A GERMAN COURTROOM. GROENING HAD BEEN CHARGED AND CONVICTED AS AN ACCESSORY TO THE MURDER OF THREE HUNDRED THOUSAND VICTIMS AS THE "BOOKKEEPER OF AUSCHWITZ". AS A CORPORAL IN THE DEATH CAMP OFFICE, HE HAD BEEN INVOLVED IN THE MANAGEMENT OF FUNDS CONFISCATED FROM PRISONERS.

EVA HUGGED AND KISSED THE NINETY-FOUR-YEAR-OLD MAN AND WENT ON TO URGE THAT HE NOT SPEND TIME IN PRISON BUT RATHER TALK TO THE YOUNG ABOUT THE TRAGEDY OF NAZISM IN THE CONVICTION THAT EDUCATION AND COMPASSION COULD STOP IT FROM EVER RISING AGAIN.

IN RESPONSE TO
CRITICISM OF HER
FORGIVENESS, SHE STATED,
"NOTHING GOOD COMES
FROM ANGER."

AN ONGOING COMPONENT OF EVA'S COMPASSIONATE EDUCATING WAS HER PILGRIMAGES TO AUSCHWITZ AND BIRKENAU.

AFTER HER FIRST CATHARTIC JOURNEY THERE IN 1985, EVA TOOK MORE THAN THIRTY TRIPS TO THE CAMPS. EACH TIME SHE TRAVELED THERE, SHE TOOK MORE AND MORE ADULTS AND STUDENTS WITH HER UNDER THE AUSPICES OF THE CANDLES MUSEUM.

WITH POLISH GUIDES AND MOST IMPORTANTLY WITH EVA HERSELF TELLING THE PILGRIMS THE CATASTROPHIC STORY OF THIS PLACE AND EVA'S PERSONAL STORY WITHIN IT.

THE INTACT GAS CHAMBER AND CREMATORIUM IN AUSCHWITZ.

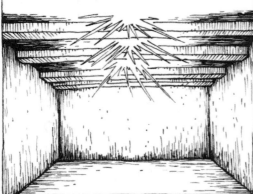

AND THE RUINS OF THE FOUR IN BIRKENAU.

THEY WOULD SEE THE BRICK BUILDINGS THAT ONCE HELD THOUSANDS OF INNOCENT VICTIMS IN AUSCHWITZ AND NOW HELD EXHIBITS TELLING THE HISTORY OF THIS PLACE AND THOSE WHO SUFFERED IN IT.

AND THE REMAINING BARRACKS IN BIRKENAU THAT WERE BUILT TO HOUSE A HUNDRED BUT INSTEAD STACKED A THOUSAND SOULS IN WHAT WAS LITTLE MORE THAN A BARN.

EVA WOULD TAKE HER COMPANIONS TO THE EMPTY SPOT WITH ONLY A HINT OF FOUNDATION REMAINING IN THE WOMEN'S CAMP OF BIRKENAU THAT HAD BEEN WHERE THE TWINS' BARRACKS HAD STOOD.

EVA TOOK SPECIAL PLEASURE STANDING IN FRONT OF THE ENLARGED PHOTOGRAPH IN ONE OF THE EXHIBITS IN AN AUSCHWITZ BARRACKS DISPLAYING MIRIAM AND HER BEING LIBERATED ON THAT COLD JANUARY DAY IN 1945. SHE DISCOVERED HER IMAGE IN THE FILM FOOTAGE THE SOVIET TROOPS HAD SHOT TO DOCUMENT THE TERRIFYING CONDITIONS AND THE REMAINING INMATES.

IN JULY 2019, EVA WAS BEGINNING HER SECOND AUSCHWITZ TRIP OF THE SUMMER. SHE HAD BEEN IN POLAND TOURING WITH A LARGE GROUP COMPRISED MOSTLY OF HIGH SCHOOL STUDENTS THE LAST WEEK OF JUNE, THE WEEK OF THE HEAT WAVE THAT HAD GRIPPED THE ENTIRETY OF EUROPE.

EVA MET THE NEW GROUP IN THE LOBBY OF THE HOTEL IN KRAKOW. GREETING, LAUGHING, AND FIST-BUMPING THE NEW ARRIVALS.

THE NEXT EVENING, SHE SHARED A MEAL IN THE HOTEL DINING ROOM AND WATCHED TED GREEN'S DOCUMENTARY, *EVA: A-7063*, WITH HER PILGRIMS OF EDUCATORS, ARTISTS, AND ADMIRERS. SHE STAYED LATE ANSWERING QUESTIONS AND TELLING STORIES.

THE GROUP SPENT THE NEXT MORNING IN BIRKENAU WITH POLISH GUIDES TELLING ITS HISTORY AND DETAILING ITS ATROCITIES. IN THE EARLY AFTERNOON, EVA JOINED THEM AFTER AN IMPROMPTU SERENADE BY THE LA CHILDREN'S CHORUS SINGING A SONG OF "SHALOM" AND EVA'S FAVORITE, "THE IMPOSSIBLE DREAM":

EVA DRESSED IN HER BLUE UNIFORM (SHE HAD SELECTED IT YEARS BEFORE TO STAND OUT FROM HER AUDIENCE AND, AS SHE JOKINGLY ADMITTED, BECAUSE IT MADE HER EYES "POP") AND CONVEYED IN HER "POPE MOBILE" WITH PILGRIMS IN TOW, PROCEEDED TO THE SELECTION PLATFORM.

EVA TOLD THE STORY OF HER LONG JOURNEY FROM ROMANIA TO AUSCHWITZ TO INDIANA, FROM DEPRESSION AND ANGER TO JOY AND FORGIVENESS, ALL IN THE SHADE OF A BOXCAR OF THE KIND THAT WOULD HAVE BROUGHT HER HERE SEVENTY-FIVE YEARS BEFORE ON THE LAST DAY SHE WOULD EVER BE WITH MAMA AND PAPA AND EDIT AND ALIZ.

AND SHE READ LETTERS OF FORGIVENESS WRITTEN TO HER PARENTS: HER FATHER'S HARSH TREATMENT OF THE DAUGHTER WHO WAS NOT A SON AND HER MOTHER'S REFUSAL TO LEAVE FOR PALESTINE WHEN THE OPPORTUNITY COULD HAVE BECOME A LIFE-SAVING REALITY. AS THE GROUP WELLED WITH EMOTION, EVA STOPPED AND, WITH CANTANKEROUS GRACE, ADDRESSED THE TEARS:

"WHY ARE YOU CRYING?

IT'S A HAPPY STORY.

I SURVIVED.

I BEAT HITLER.

I BEAT MENGELE.

I BEAT THE NAZIS.

I BEAT THE COMMUNISTS.

AND I AM HERE TO TELL MY STORY."

EARLY THE NEXT MORNING, JULY 4, 2019, THE USA's INDEPENDENCE DAY, EVA, WHO HAD BECOME A PROUD AMERICAN CITIZEN IN 1965, DIED WITH HER SON, ALEX, WHO HAD ACCOMPANIED HER ON MANY JOURNEYS, BY HER SIDE. THE FOLLOWING SATURDAY AT THE STARK MEMORIAL SCULPTURE BETWEEN THE RUINS OF BIRKENAU'S GAS CHAMBERS II AND III, A SMALL SERVICE WAS HELD: THE KADDISH WAS RECITED, "THE IMPOSSIBLE DREAM" WAS SUNG, CANDLES WERE LIGHTED, AND A WREATH PLACED. A RIBBON ADORNING THE WREATH SIMPLY STATED: * SHE LIVED. SHE SURVIVED. SHE FORGAVE. EVA"

EVA MOZES KOR IS GONE, BUT HER STORY, THE STORY OF ALL THE VICTIMS OF THE NAZIS, ALL THE VICTIMS OF OPPRESSION WHEREVER THEY HAPPEN MUST BE TOLD, RETOLD. KNOWING LEADS TO NEVER REPEATING THE CRIMES OF THE PAST, AND EVA'S FORGIVENESS IS THE BALM THAT HEALS THE INJURED SOUL.

TELL THE STORY
AND FORGIVE.

JOE LEE is a cartoonist, illustrator, writer, and former circus clown. He is the author/illustrator of books on clowns, Dante, and Greek mythology; editorial cartoonist for the Bloomington *Herald-Times*; and staff illustrator for *Our Brown County Magazine*. His latest large work is the LeGrande Circus & Sideshow Tarot for US Games. Lee is a graduate of Indiana University and is currently based in Bloomington, Indiana.